Unless the Tongue Catch Fire

Homilies on Ministry

Unless the Tongue Catch Fire

Homilies on Ministry

Archbishop George Stack

GRACEWING

First published in 2015

Gracewing
2 Southern Avenue
Leominster
Herefordshire HR6 0QF

ISBN 978 0 85244 845 8

Typeset by Action Publishing Technology Ltd
Gloucester GL1 5SR

Contents

Introduction

One of the many beautiful themes addressed by Pope Francis in his Apostolic Exhortation *Evangelii Gaudium* is the importance of preaching. Not just its importance, but the nature of the dialogue which takes place between God and his people during the homily. By way of preparation, the Pope invites the one who is ordained to minister the Word and Sacrament to share prayerfully with his people '. . . what does this text say *to me*? What is it about my life that you wish to be changed by this text? What troubles me about this text? Why am I not interested in this? . . . What is it about this word that moves me?' (Par. 153)

These words re-affirm what bishops, priests and deacons know. That preaching is an intensely personal experience which has enormous public significance. The engagement between the preacher and the listener is truly 'Heart speaking to heart' in the many different circumstances of life. Whilst addressing the deepest needs of the human heart, the homily '. . . surpasses all forms of catechesis as the supreme moment in the dialogue between God and his people which lead up to sacramental communion'. (Par. 137)

This short book of homilies is being published in response to the common request made of many preachers for a copy of their homily. I have delayed the publication since I believe the experience of giving and receiving a homily is an extraordinarily personal one both for the preacher and the listener. It is deeply affected by the circumstances of the liturgy and the engagement of the people. All who preach experience the privilege of the sacred space they occupy in the hearts and minds of those who are attentive to the word of God.

The homilies are dedicated to the deacons and priests at whose ordinations I have been privileged to preside. As preachers, they will have reflected on the words in the Letter to the Romans: 'Faith comes from what is heard, and what is heard comes by the preaching of Christ'. (Rom. 10:17) Those who know me will be aware of my belief that often it is through the symbolic language of poetry that the deep truths of faith can be embraced in our imagination. Hence they will not be surprised that I have chosen as the title of this collection of homilies a line from William Blake's poem 'The Fourfold Vision' which captures, for me, the dynamic of the word spoken and the word heard in the ministry of preaching:

Unless the eye catch fire
The God will not be seen.
Unless the ear catch fire
The God will not be heard.
Unless the tongue catch fire
The God will not be named.
Unless the heart catch fire
The God will not be loved.
Unless the mind catch fire
The God will not be known.

+ George Stack
Archbishop of Cardiff

Fr Gerard Skinner
First Mass
21 July 2002

First Reading: Wisdom 12:13–19
Second Reading: Romans 8:26–27
Gospel: Matthew 13:24–30

> It was the best of times;
> it was the worst of times.
> It was the age of wisdom;
> it was the age of foolishness.
> It was the epoch of belief;
> it was the epoch of incredulity.
> It was the season of Light;
> it was the season of Darkness.
> It was the spring of hope;
> it was the winter of despair.
> We had everything before us;
> we had nothing before us.
> We were all going direct to Heaven;
> we were all going direct the other way.

Not an analysis of religion and culture in the Britain of the twenty-first century, but the opening words of *A Tale of Two Cities* by Charles Dickens. It is yet another reminder that every society, in every age, finds it difficult to read the signs of its own time.

When the People of Israel entered the Promised Land they were confused and disappointed. They found the land already occupied by the Canaanites. Much of the Old Testament Book of Numbers describes the battles they fought to take possession of the land. In their turmoil, they complained to Moses: If God had promised them this land, why was their struggle for it so demanding, confusing and conflict ridden? With the hindsight of history, and the benefit of faith, the people were eventually able to say the prayer we heard in this morning's extract from the Book of Wisdom:

> By acting thus you have taught a lesson to your people:
> How the virtuous man must be kindly to his fellow man.
> And you have given your sons hope,
> That after sin you will grant repentance.

If our ancestors faced a crisis of faith as they tried to comprehend their complex world, how much more true is it for us today. The exploration of science and advances in technology could be seen as unfolding the mystery of creation – or exploding the myth.

The development of medical ethics enabling us to hold back disease and death create extraordinary moral dilemmas, not least the price we pay in the dehumanisation of life. What is legal is not necessarily moral!

Economic development and wealth creation are essential constituents of our global village. But the price being paid in the widening gap between 'rich' and 'poor' is simply not sustainable. The churches are taking the lead not just in helping the victims of poverty but challenging the unjust structures, which make people poor.

The multicultural, multi-faith society in which our new priest will work demands a fresh presentation of Jesus as the unique revelation of God, the one who brings salvation. The dialogue with Hindu, Muslim and Jew about the truth of their religious experience, and ours, now has a direct impact on what goes on in the streets of the inner cities.

> It really is the best of times and the worst of times.
> It is an age of faith, it is an age of incredulity.
> It is a spring of hope. It is a winter of despair.

That duality of faith lived out in a world of conflict and confusion is described marvellously in today's extract from the Gospel of Matthew. Wheat and weeds growing in the field together. Difficult for us to identify what is of real and what is of long-term value. Impossible to weed if, in doing so, damage could be done to what is good, true, honest and authentic in our own lives as well as our complex society. The Church itself, described by Vatican II as 'a divine and human interlocked reality', contains extraordinary, heroic goodness and damaging, painful, sin.

In a world of creative tension and contradictions, our new priest must be a sign of contradiction himself. At his ordination yesterday he promised obedience to his Bishop and to the People of God. In a world which says freedom and independence are the absolute ultimate values, the person who makes a gift of that freedom for the glory of God and service of his people really has to become 'a fool for Christ's sake'.

He was asked: 'Will you unite yourself more closely to Christ the High Priest who offered Himself as a perfect sacrifice to the Father?'

The Cross of Jesus Christ stands at the crossroads of human history. No trees, no wheat, no flowers grew on Calvary, only dead wood and weeds. Where is God in the midst of human turmoil and suffering? 'Here', says Jesus with arms outstretched on the Cross. The lowest point of human history becomes the highest point of God's revelation. The definitive moment of true worship of God came when all the circumstances pointed to the contrary.

Gerard will re-present that mystery as he celebrates the Mass and conforms his life to the Cross of Jesus Christ.

Some people will see the gift of his young life to the priesthood as a waste of his undoubted talent. But he is content to work in the Lord's complex field and plant the harvest and help it grow in faith and dedication. In his priesthood he will do what he can to fulfil the final words of Jesus in today's gospel extract: 'At the harvest time the virtuous will shine like the sun in the kingdom of the Father. Listen, anyone who has ears to hear.'

Canon Daniel Cronin
Induction as New Parish Priest, Hampstead
14 October 2001

First Reading: 2 Kings 5:14–17
Second Reading: 2 Timothy 2:8–13
Gospel: Luke 17:11–19

I am always moved when I see the Pope making one of his missionary journeys. On arriving in a new country, he would kneel down and kiss the soil. Now he is so fragile, the earth is presented to him in two bowls which he honours with a kiss. In that gesture he marks the sacredness of the land. In that action he is doing honour to its people.

Nine hundred years before Christ, Naaman, a nobleman, a general, a Syrian, was desperate for a cure from what we today call leprosy. He had tried everything to be cured. In desperation he went to the prophet in Israel called Elisha. The prophet told Naaman to do the simplest thing. Go and wash in the River Jordan. Against his better judgement, Naaman passed the test of faith. He did what he was told. He wasn't just healed. He was converted: 'I know that there is no other God but the God of Israel.' And what did he do? He loaded two containers of soil from the land of Israel on his donkeys to take back home. And why? So that he could worship God on the sacred soil of Israel.

In today's gospel passage we learn that the contagious nature of leprosy was bad enough. As well as being mortally ill, they were ritually unclean. One consequence of this was that the sufferers were ostracised. 'They stood some way off and shouted'. The most painful isolation was the fact that they were forbidden to join the community in worship in the Temple. Hence the instruction, 'Go and show yourself to the priest.' Go and prove yourself worthy of joining the worshipping community. So, because of the double significance of this healing, perhaps we can better understand the meaning of the sadness in the words of Jesus: 'no one came back to praise God except this foreigner.'

Is it possible to make a connection between these readings and the induction of your new parish priest? I think there is. Because above all the task of the priest is to empower people to worship God, to give praise to God, in every circumstance of life. But worship God in his way, not in ours.

In his preaching, the priest presents reasons for which we should thank God. He reminds us to take nothing for granted. He challenges us never to lose sight of the things of heaven by being too preoccupied with the things of the earth.

In his pastoral duties, particularly in his care of the sick and the needy, he will share your sadness and pain. One horrendous result of leprosy is that the sufferer could feel no pain. Part of the cure in today's Gospel must surely be they now could feel pain. There is no person, no family, no parish that does not experience sadness, loneliness, suffering, ultimately death. The task of the priest is to sustain people in their pain, to help them grow through the cross.

The hill of Calvary became Holy Ground through the sacrifice of Himself, which Jesus offered on the Cross. We, too, stand on holy ground in this church as we re-member, re-present that sacrifice in the Holy Communion we celebrate and receive through the ministry of your priest.

Fr James Garvey
Induction as Parish Priest
St Bernadette's, Hillingdon
2 February 2002

Earlier today we celebrated the Feast of the Presentation of Our Lord, commonly known as Candlemas Day. Among other things, the feast marks the completion of Christmas since it occurs forty days after Christmas. It also anticipates the feast of Easter with the forty days of Lent looming up ahead of us. The feast of Christmas and the feast of Easter are linked by the light of a candle which we use today. The candle symbolises 'Christ, Our Light'. It reminds all of us that we, too, must be lights in a darkened world.

But this evening we keep the fourth Ordinary Sunday of the Church's year. Except, of course, no Sunday is ordinary. In fact, our celebration of Sunday is quite extraordinary. Why? Because the history of salvation, the story of God's revelation, the experience of God's forgiveness and presence among us is proclaimed, celebrated, presented as a challenge in our journey of faith Sunday after Sunday.

I use the word 'presented' to us. But the reality is that it is represented during our Sunday Mass. Jesus re-presented by the one ordained, ordered, directed to remember, re-member, put back together again, the broken body of Christ at this time, in this parish, in the lives of people he is called to serve.

One reason for the solemn Induction of a Parish Priest is to remind us that his is not just a function. He is not just an administrator, or a school governor, or a keeper of buildings. He is the one who was called to be an *alter Christus* in your midst. He is supposed to be an icon of Christ, a sacrament, a sign that the servant Christ is present among you.

That is why certain words and actions are performed during this ceremony. The new parish priest is given the keys to the church. Keys speak of authority. They speak about responsibility for the fabric. They remind him that he has to be close to the author of all truth. He looks after a church in this parish certainly. But more importantly he looks after the Church, which is the Body of Christ.

He will be seated in the chair. Not just any old chair. But it is called the *Presider's Chair*. It is a reminder that the one who sits there is the head of the Body of Christ in this place. Without a priest there is no Eucharistic community. He brings together all the parts of that body and unifies them in holy communion. Not because he is better, or cleverer, or holier than Catholics in his parish. But he is ordered, directed, ordained to the task of service and remembrance.

He is taken to the lectern where he will preach the word of God. He should always remember that the preacher should speak to God's people with the bible in one hand and the newspaper in the other. It is his task to bring together those two worlds. This evening we listened to the most profound sermon of all – the Sermon on the Mount. In those beatitudes we hear the essence of the teaching of Jesus Christ. It has been called the Christians' Charter.

But the one who preaches knows that he is not just speaking words. His life of service, his ministry and his priesthood are sermons in action.

At the Offertory of this Mass gifts of bread and wine are brought to the priest. We call them fruits of human effort, labour. These are acknowledgements of our dependence on God. We give thanks to God for what we have and what we are and we pray to God for what we might become. We pray that these gifts of bread and wine are changed into the body and blood of Jesus Christ. We pray that we ourselves may be changed into people worthy of bearing his name. They are a token, a symbol, of our whole lives. They are received and transformed and changed into the body and blood of Jesus. His is the complete worship of God – the offering of the whole of his life, even unto death.

At Mass we receive Holy Communion with the Body of Christ, and it is indeed, an intensely personal experience and an expression of faith. But equally important is the fact that we become holy 'com-union', with and for, each other. The Body of Christ is really present where two or three are gathered in his name. By receiving Jesus in holy communion, we are expressing that fundamental unity which exists between all believers. In that vertical and horizontal relationship which is true communion, we can fulfil the command of Paul that we bear one another's burdens. (Gal. 6:2) This is what should go on in every parish. The strong are given something to strive for whilst the weak are not oppressed and over-burdened. The task of the priest is to facilitate the various members of the body fulfilling their different roles, ministries and potential for the glory of God and the salvation of the world. It is to this noble work that your parish priest dedicates himself anew today.

Mark Vickers
Diaconate Ordination
6 April 2002

If ever we needed reminding of the significance of ritual, ceremony and liturgy in life, we only have to observe the events surrounding the death and funeral of the Queen Mother this week. Some people will derive great comfort from those rituals. Others will take pride in memories or national identity. But as well as being a great act of thanksgiving, the unifying force of those ceremonies is surely the honouring of values which transcend the here and now, values personified in that special life.

Most people describe the life as one of devotion to duty; a life given to service; a life of generosity and love. Without taking the funereal theme too far, are not these excellent descriptions of the Diaconate and of all Holy Orders? We heard them described in different language in the reading from the Acts of the Apostles: the early Church needed men of good reputation. Wise men. Men filled with the Spirit of God who could be of service to God's people. (Acts 6:1–7) 'After enquiry among the people of God, this man, your brother Mark Vickers, has been found to have these qualities. He has been found worthy'.

The service of God and his people can only be offered with a generous heart and a love-filled life. Love for everybody, not just one person. The gift of celibacy is precisely that: your gift to God of love, intimacy, of life's longing for itself. And why? So that in a very public way you can build up that civilisation of love which is the kingdom of God. Celibacy is also God's gift to you, filling heart and life itself with his divine intimacy, which is prayer – the adventure of love.

When you lie prostrate on the ground in a moment, this will be a sign of your abandonment to the power and love of God. It is a gesture of emptying of self so that God will fill you with his power, his presence, his love, so that you in turn may be a living witness of his love among the people you serve. And you are not alone. Surrounded by family and friends, you will also be supported and inspired by a cloud of heavenly witnesses who have achieved the holiness you and I are seeking.

The promise of obedience to your Bishop is another external sign of an inner gift. Obedience demands faith and it demands trust. Believing that God speaks in and through his Church. Not an imposition, restricting our freedom. Cardinal Hume said often: 'Once you have given yourself in obedience, you have nothing to lose. Everything is freedom.'

This ordination takes place 'By the Prayer of the Church and the laying on of hands.' That extraordinarily powerful gesture which signifies the calling down of God's spirit at this time, in this place, on this person. You will perform that gesture yourself, Mark, in Baptism, and as a priest when you consecrate, when you forgive, when you anoint the sick. The prayer of ordination and the laying on of hands links the one who is ordained to the ministry of the apostles who 'laid hands on them'.

And then you are clothed in Dalmatic and stole. Extraordinary garments. Whether it's a Dalmatic, a chasuble or mitre, these vestments remind us we are not performing these sacred actions because we are clever, or holy, or better than others. These vestments cover our weakness, our idiosyncracies, our limitations. It is a good thing that our people know, even if we forget, that when we put on our vestments we are clothed in Christ, acting in his name, for the service of his people, and not just purveying our own version of reality.

The ordination of a Deacon concludes with the presentation of the Book of the Gospels, the living Word of God on whom your life is based and from whom you will draw inspiration and strength to preach to others what you have learned and what you live yourself. You will know already that preaching God's word doesn't just take place in the pulpit, but in your heart and in your life. The words used at this presentation are both a comfort and a challenge. 'Believe what you read. Teach what you believe. Practice what you teach.' And be assured of the Prayer of the Church on this day of ordination and in the years of service ahead.

Nicholas Schofield
Diaconate Ordination
29 June 2002

First Reading: Acts 3:1–10
Second Reading: Galatians 2:11–14
Gospel: John 21:15–19

There is a beautiful hymn written for this feast of St Peter and St Paul. Unfortunately, it is rarely sung because people find the tune too difficult to learn. The second verse of the hymn is very special:

> One taught mankind its creed, one guards the heavenly gate.
> Founders of Rome, they bind the world in loyalty.
> One by the sword achieved, one by the cross his fate.
> With laurelled brows they hold eternal royalty.

Memory and poetry have a tendency to conflate or gloss over the lives of historic characters, even saintly ones. You only have to read today's scripture passage to the Christians in Galatia to realise that the relationship between Peter and Paul was not an easy one. Paul the educated, articulate, passionate convert. Peter the fisherman, the one who bides his time, a bit laid back, given to the easy option. There had already been one major disagreement in Jerusalem. And now, when Peter came to Antioch Paul 'opposed him to his face' because of hypocrisy. Peter was happy to eat with pagan converts to Christianity when there were no Jewish converts around. But when James and the strict Jews came from Jerusalem, Peter withdrew from the Gentile converts just to keep the peace.

These were the growing pains of the early Church. Different interpretations and understanding of authority. Deciding what was essential discipline and changing practice. Whatever the difficulties, the apostles and disciples were united in their faith in Jesus Christ, in his risen presence and in his transforming effect in the lives of all who believed in him.

Each one of us ordained to minister in word and sacrament has been touched by those same fundamental truths. Each of us brings his own special gifts and insight, his unique personality to the service of the Gospel. At the same time, each of us is only a small part of the overall scheme of things. Our particular insight or understanding is part of a greater whole.

Perhaps this is what Peter meant when he said to the cripple at the Beautiful Gate, 'What I have I give you'. What can our new Deacon give to the people who come, not to the Beautiful Gate, but to the presbytery door, to the school gates, who come to the hospital, or come in any need whatsoever. You only have one thing to give Nicholas. You give your personal faith in Jesus Christ. And the authority entrusted to you by the Church is a sign of God's faith in you. When people ask you to pray for them, and with them, you are fulfilling that personal and public responsibility. That is why you are asked: Will you maintain and deepen a spirit of prayer not just for your own needs, but for the glory of God and the well-being of his people?

Three times in the Gospel Jesus asks Peter, 'Do you love me?' Is it too much to say that the questions put to Nicholas during his ordination are the gentle probing by Jesus of the heart and soul of the person who is to be ordained?

- Are you resolved to exercise your diaconal service with humility and love?
- Are you resolved to hold the mystery of faith taught by the apostles?
- Is the obedience you promise a grudging acceptance of authority, or is it the sign of freedom born of a wholehearted faith, hope and love for the Church which is Christ's Body whom you will serve?

'I am. I do. I will, with the help of God.'

Lord, you know that I love you. That is why I am setting aside a career, and money and material goods. You know I love you. That is why I am making a gift of my right to intimacy and marriage and a family of my own to live in the celibate state as a sign of the other values to be embraced in your kingdom. You know I love you. That is why I am promising obedience. Like Peter, I am prepared to go where I would not choose. I will do all in my power to raise people up, to bring them to the Temple, to help them praise and thank and worship God with the totality of their lives.

'Feed my lambs. Take care of my sheep.'

'May God who began the good work in you bring it to fulfilment.'

And then the wordless language and power of the sacrament takes over. You prostrate yourself on the ground before God and abandon yourself to *his* love. The Laying on of Hands and Prayer of Consecration express many truths, but ultimately God's faith in you. The Deacon's stole over your shoulder. 'My yoke is easy and my burden light'. You are giving the gift of your young life to God and his Church. The sacred belt put over your shoulder is a sign of authority and service. It is a burden and a delight. It will give you privileged access into the lives of people and places and situations.

> 'Receive the Gospel of Christ whose herald you
> now are . . .'

You will already have learned in Harlesden, but will experience it even more powerfully as a Deacon, that the sermons you preach are not just with words, and are not just in this pulpit. The best sermon is the quality of your life, the consistency of your prayer, and the service you offer, today and for the rest of your life.

Commissioning of Catechists, Readers and Eucharistic Ministers Our Lady & St Bridget, Isleworth 13 October 2002

I returned from Rome last Friday having been there for a week to take part in two quite different events.

For the last few days I attended a conference to celebrate the tenth anniversary of the publication of the *Catechism of the Catholic Church*. This was not a celebration in the usual sense. Lectures from 9.00 in the morning until 7.30 in the evening with a two-hour break for lunch! But it was very interesting to hear Bishops and Catechists from all over the world explaining the issues they are facing in their own countries in handing on the faith. It's that Tradition, that handing on of something precious, something beautiful, something that will give meaning and purpose to our lives in this world and the next which is the key to all catechesis. And, of course, it is not *what* we pass on which is important. It is *who* we pass on, the person of Jesus Christ, present among us in time and in history, in word and in sacrament, in community and fellowship and care for one another. This 'handing on' takes place in that complex reality which is the Church, the Body of Christ, in this place, amongst these people, at this complex point in history.

The Pope told us that Christ is the teacher. We are the disciples. The word 'disciple' means 'the one who listens'. It's difficult to hear in the noisy world and the lives we lead. Christ speaks to us in different ways. In the silence of our hearts. In our prayer. During the Mass. In the preaching by the priest. In study of the Bible. Through the demands of others. We need to be attentive to his word. That word is articulated for us in the words of catechists in the parish. The Pope again said: 'Catechesis is the responsibility of the whole Church, but certain members of the Church exercise that responsibility in a special way, through training and commitment and dedication to the service of teaching the faith.' That is why we have a special act of commissioning and dedication, because our catechists undertake this responsibility and privilege in your name and in mine.

The second event for which I was present in Rome was the canonisation of a new saint: Josemaria Escriva. He died only twenty-seven years ago. Whatever the controversies about him, he proclaimed a radical truth: that true holiness, true happiness, true fulfilment in life comes in serving God in our career, in the world of work, in our family life. He wrote that he wanted people to find God in the middle of ordinary things: he wanted a tailor saint, an office saint, a factory saint, an architect saint, a husband saint, a wife saint. His books called *The Way* and *Christ is Passing By* have been an inspiration to the members of the organisation he founded called Opus Dei, the Work of God.

Those of you who read the word of God and minister the Body of Christ are making real the truth that it is when two or three are gathered in the name of Jesus, he is there among us. The reading of the Bible, the teaching of the faith, the distribution of the Body of Christ are not just mechanical actions. By your very presence you are ministering Christ to others, you are making him present to them by the very service you perform. It is true that in communion we are united with Jesus in a profound and sacramental way, one to one. But that vertical communion between the individual and God has to be expressed and sustained through the holy communion, the fellowship, the care and the responsibility which we exercise for each other through our parish, through our priest and through our ministers of word and sacrament. It could be described as the horizontal dimension of communion.

You will have heard that the Cardinal is taking all the priests away in a month's time to explore with them how they can better build up the Body of Christ by empowering people to know better the Word of God who is Jesus Christ, to deepen their relationship with him through prayer and the sacraments, and to strengthen the communities of faith to which we belong so that people can say 'How these Christians love one another.' In this act of dedication and commitment, this parish is anticipating all that the Cardinal wants - parishes, Diocese and a Church composed of people who hear the word of God and act on it for the glory of God and the well-being of his people everywhere.

Allen Hall
Mass for Candidacy
Feast of the Douay Martyrs
27 October 2002

Next time you pass Westminster Abbey look at the archway over the main entrance. Five years ago the Queen unveiled those statues of twelve martyrs of the twentieth century. Amongst them are Maximilian Kolbe and Archbishop Luwum of Uganda. More controversially, there are statues of Martin Luther King and Dietrich Bonhoeffer. A very special one for me is the statue of Archbishop Oscar Romero, who was shot in the head as he elevated the consecrated host at Mass.

He knew he was in danger of assassination because of his defence of the poor of El Salvador. Interviewed by journalists in the March before he was killed he said:

> I have been threatened with death many times, but I say as a Christian I am not afraid of death. I believe in Resurrection. If they kill me, I will rise again in the Salvadorian people . . . A Bishop will die, but the Church of God, which is the people, will never perish.

I love the phrase: 'The blood of the martyrs is the seedbed of the Church.' This has been proved down through the ages from the martyrdom of Stephen in the Acts of the Apostles, through our own martyrs of Douay whose memory we keep today, down to the Dominican Bishop of Oran. The story of martyrdom is that you can kill the messenger but the message will never be extinguished. Because the martyr is one who witnesses to truths which lie beyond any human control or restriction.

The martyr is one who can give his or her life simply because they possess their identity completely.

Take one of our own martyrs of Douay, St John Southworth, whose shrine is in Westminster Cathedral. Born in 1592, he prepared for the priesthood in Douay but at times felt called to the Benedictine life. He was eventually ordained for the English mission in 1624. In deciding where to work, we read, 'Two areas were notorious for papists: the warren of back alleys in the parish of St Giles Holborn, and the west end of the parish of Saint Margaret's, Westminster, which scarcely deserved even the designation of a slum.' (That's the area around Westminster Cathedral. Some people think things haven't changed much!)

If you visit his shrine in the Cathedral, read about his twenty years of work in our Diocese, ministering to the victims of the plague in 1636. Read also about his refusal to deny his priesthood, even though the judge said there was no proof that he was a priest. John Southworth thought that a change of plea would be a scandal to the poor Catholics he had served all those years.

Southworth, and all our martyrs of Douay, was a witness to Christ both in his life and in his death. And it is in the light of that same faith and witness that a new generation of men today offer themselves as candidates for the same service, the same diaconate and priesthood, the same Mass for which John Southworth gave his life. In being accepted as candidates for ordination, the Apostolic Letter of Pope Paul VI tells each of you 'to care for your vocation in a special way and deepen it. You will also acquire the right to the necessary spiritual assistance by which your vocation must be developed and be submitted unconditionally to the love of God.'

The martyr, the witness, the one who is a candidate for ordination, submits his life unconditionally to the love of

God. And none of us knows where that unconditional commitment will lead us. There will be times when we will want to hold on to our life, hold on to our views, hold on to our own way of doing things. But if we are to be authentic witnesses and servants of the Gospel we must *give* our lives to the enterprise for the glory of God and to the people.

I am sorry that the reading from the martyrdom of the Maccabean brothers finished at verse 14. In verse 20 we read of the encouragement which the mother gives to her seven sons. We are told:

> . . . the mother was especially admirable and worthy of mention . . . because of her hope in the Lord . . . she encouraged each of them in the language of their ancestors. Filled with noble conviction she reinforced her womanly argument with manly courage. (2 Macc 7:20–21)

None of us who are ministers of word and sacrament can sustain this life on our own. We need encouragement, example, prayers and support of the people we serve. Our candidates for future ordination have already experienced the dynamic of mutual support which is given and received in the proper service of people. Only with the help of witnessing the heroic struggle in the lives of people you serve will you in turn be able to personify in lives of heroic witness the greatest commandment of all: Love God with all your heart, with all your soul, with all your mind. And love your neighbour as you love yourself. Now *there's* a martyrdom, *there's* a heroic witness, worth living for and in which to die.

Cardinal Cormac Murphy-O'Connor, Bishops James O'Brien and Philip Harvey Episcopal Silver Jubilee 14 December 2002

First Reading: Isaiah 61:1–3
Gospel: Luke 5:1–11

On the day of his ordination, the new Bishop is questioned in an age-old and searching way about the ministry he is about to undertake. He is asked:

> Will you be faithful and constant in proclaiming the Gospel of Christ?
> Will you show kindness and compassion to the poor, the stranger, to all who are in need?
> Will you sustain God's people and guide them in the way of salvation?

He is reminded that 'the title of Bishop is one not of honour, but of function and, therefore, the Bishop should strive to serve rather than to rule'.

There is no doubt that each of our Bishops has fulfilled those instructions in the last twenty-five years. Cardinal Cormac first as Bishop of Arundel and Brighton, and now as Archbishop of Westminster with diocesan, national and international responsibilities. Bishop James O'Brien as a devoted Area Bishop in Hertfordshire and through his commitment to ecumenical work in the Diocese and beyond. Bishop Philip Harvey, the much-loved Area

Bishop in North London and his extraordinary expertise in the social and welfare work of the Church.

The word 'Jubilee' is very much in our minds as we celebrate these anniversaries. Nowhere is Jubilee better explained than in the letter of Pope John Paul II in preparation for the Jubilee of the Year 2000. The Pope meditates on the text from the prophet Isaiah to which we have just listened. Isaiah is the voice of Advent because he is the one who proclaims 'the fullness of time' at the coming of the Messiah.

The Pope writes that Jubilee turns the normal pattern of life upside down. The poor hear good news. Those who are broken are to be healed, sustained, renewed. Those who are trapped in external or internal prisons can be given hope. The task of the Church under the leadership of its Bishop is not merely to comfort the downtrodden but also confront structures of injustice, to name the issues, to commit the Church and its people to alternative ways of living, to help them create the 'civilisation of love' spoken of by Pope Paul VI. Hope is an Advent word.

In order to be signs of hope we must surely listen to God's word with new ears. The word of God, not just read, not just spoken, but the word of God made flesh in Jesus Christ. That word speaks to us through scripture and tradition. It speaks through our shared faith in the community of believers. The word speaks in the gift of Jesus in the Eucharist. Peter said, 'At your word, Lord, I will put down the nets'. His experience taught him otherwise. 'We have worked all night and caught nothing.' But hearing God's word in a different way, Peter was prepared to trust. That trust taught him that *his* own way was not the only way. Because he was open to new possibilities, the result was a huge catch of fish.

Hope and trust are not just Advent themes. They are the essence of our relationship with God and also with our

Bishop. Whilst Jubilees look back and give thanks to God for the past twenty-five years, they also celebrate the present reality and look to the future. The experience of 'putting out into the deep' in the last few weeks, has been an extraordinary one for the Diocese under the leadership of the Cardinal. The great deanery gatherings that we have had show a richness and enthusiasm for our faith in the parishes of our diocese. They show a readiness for spiritual and pastoral renewal. They show a desire to be of service in new ways, perhaps yet unknown. They show the courage of our bishop to explore ways of 'being church' and his willingness to be with us in 'consulting the laity' not just in words but in action.

The universal call to holiness of all God's people is spelt out in the decree on the Church of the Second Vatican Council. The people of God is a priestly people. We worship God not merely as individuals, but as the body of Christ. We share Christ's role as a prophet, speaking, acting, working out the things of God in human ways. The bishop is called to be the focus of unity in all this. 'Are you resolved to build up the Church, the body of Christ, and remain united with it?'

The Cardinal may not use quite the same language as St Paul, or see the responsibilities of administration as being an act of mercy. But we would surely agree with Paul that there has been no weakening in his dedication. Loyalty, fidelity, humour, service, encouragement, trust. These are the qualities we have experienced and continue to experience from our Cardinal Cormac, Bishop James and Bishop Philip Harvey.

Through their twenty-five years as bishops they will have surely meditated on the words of a great bishop of the fourth century, St Augustine:

> When I am frightened by what I am to you
> I am consoled by what I am with you.
> To you, I am the Bishop
> With you, I am a Christian
> The first is an office, the second a grace.
> The first a danger, the second salvation.

Be consoled by our loyalty and support. Be encouraged by our love and affection. Be assured that the people of this Diocese are prepared to 'launch out into the deep' under your leadership and at the Word of the Lord.

Mgr George Tancred Memorial Mass St James', Twickenham 23 December 2002

First Reading: Wisdom 3:1–9
Gospel: John 17:24–26

During this season of Advent we prepare to celebrate the coming of Christ in history. The celebration of Christmas is the feast of the Incarnation. Advent is a season of love. We also look forward to his coming at the end of time. The Old Testament prophecies are full of expectation, judgment and hope. But we are convinced that the end of time is now. Every moment of every day is the end of that time. Jesus is present among us here and now as we come together in faith and as we receive him in Word and Sacrament. Advent is a multi-faceted reality for those who believe.

Do you remember the First Sunday of Advent? Stay awake. Stand ready. For you do not know either the day or the hour of his coming. I suppose it is only when somebody close to us dies that those words take on a whole new and urgent meaning. During this Advent I have lost somebody to whom I was close, through a tragic accident. Those words have spoken to me with a new and powerful urgency. And now we are mourning the sudden loss of a greatly loved and respected priest.

We have good reason to give thanks for the life and ministry of Mgr George Tancred. Just reading his Diocesan obituary gives an indication of the richness and depth of his life: Educated at the English College, Lisbon and ordained in 1958 for the diocese of Salford. Appointed Spiritual Director at Ushaw College from 1972 until 1979. A whole generation of priests in the North of England have good reason to be grateful for his guidance. A period at the Cathedral in Salford followed by parish priest at Pendelton, during which he was involved in the Council of Christians and Jews as well as Vicar for Religious in the Diocese. In 1991 he was incardinated into the Diocese of Westminster and in 1992 came to St James', Twickenham. As Vicar General at that time, I was responsible in a small way for that appointment. I know that in many ways this was the happiest time of his life. There have been a number of letters from the parish telling of his influence for good on the young, his warmth and friendliness and his capacity to reconcile people to the Church.

Even on his retirement to Ireland through ill health he continued with pastoral ministry, either working as part-time chaplain at the local hospital, being involved with the Cistercian monastery at Mellafont and the local parish. Many other people have good reason to be grateful for the life and work of George Tancred.

The readings for our memorial Mass are well chosen. The Old Testament Book of Wisdom speaks of the virtuous as all those who listen to the Word of God and try to put it into practice in their lives. Written just 100 years before the time of Jesus, it is virtually the last book of the Old Testament, the Hebrew Bible. I love the phrase, 'As sparks run through the stubble, so will they'. I think of George's enthusiasm for life, his love of the theatre, his mischievous smile. Sparky. Like gold in a furnace. Full of life. Full of love for the things of God and for God's people.

I was delighted that you chose a section from the

priestly prayer of Christ from St John's Gospel. John puts these words into the lips and heart of Jesus on the night before he died, at the Last Supper. 'Father, I have known you, and these have known you, and these have known that you have sent me.' The priest is one who gets to know the Father through the priesthood he exercises and the relationship he has with Jesus the Suffering Servant. 'I have made your name known to them and I will continue to make it known'. In his preaching, in his care of the sick, in his service of the people of this parish and beyond, Fr. George sought to make the name of God known and loved to those whom he met.

It might seem strange that we are holding this Memorial Mass so close to Christmas. But I wanted it to be close to his funeral so that we might be united in prayer with those who were present at those last rites. I also wanted it to be close to the feast of the Incarnation, the birth of the Lord in whom George believed and whom he served so well. Christmas is the feast of God's love for all people, at all times, in all circumstances. It is for each in our own way to echo the prayer of love proclaimed by Jesus in his own Priestly Prayer, 'so that the love with which you loved me may be in them, and so that I may be in them'. The fact that so many have gathered at such short notice, at such a busy time of the year, is a testament that in this man, this priest, George Tancred, you caught a glimpse of the love of God made visible in Jesus Christ.

Fr Mark Vickers
First Mass
Feast of the Epiphany 2003

In the year 1913 the famous psychoanalyst Carl Jung broke his personal and professional relationship with his friend and colleague Sigmund Freud. The causes of the breakdown were complex, as you would expect from analysts. But one reason was their fundamental disagreement as to the spiritual foundation of human existence and experience. An important element in Jung's psychoanalytical theory was his work on dreams and symbols, imagery and archetypes, the connection between our inner world and the transcendent. Jung used sacramental language in a psychological world.

Whether you believe in his theory of dreams or not, there is no doubt that dreams have a great pedigree in the Bible. The Christmas and Epiphany story are interwoven with dreams. Matthew tells us that the angel of the Lord appeared to Joseph 'in a dream' following the Annunciation and told him to accept Mary as his wife. The wise men were told 'in a dream' not to return to Herod. Once more, Joseph was told 'in a dream' first to take the child down to Egypt and then to return to the land of Israel after the death of Herod.

Between the Gospel of Matthew and the insights of Carl Jung there is surely a lesson for us all. Perhaps God communicates to us 'in a dream' because of the complexities of life, because of the barriers we create, because of the sophistication which at times seeks to exclude him from the unfolding world in which we live. No accident, I think, that it is in contemplative prayer, sometimes in mysticism, perhaps only in our hopes and dreams that we are brought close to the transcendent, brought close to the truths about ourselves and our relationship with God. Hard-headed consciousness is perhaps not the best atmosphere in which we allow God access to our inner selves.

The wise men dreamed their dreams and had their visions. They came 'from the east', from unknown places, from different categories and cultures, with different histories, traditions, insights and understandings. Is it too much to say that one of the challenges facing church and society in our own day is to begin to understand what is happening 'in the east'? Not just on the international map but in the multi-cultural, multi-ethnic and multi-faith city in which we live. The parish of Kingsbury Green and the London Borough of Brent are a laboratory in which our new priest will engage with those 'from the east' who have different perspectives on the epiphany revelation. Communication with them is surely the basis of building that 'civilisation of love' which is the key to the social, racial and religious tolerance so desperately needed in our own day. And all in the context of our belief in the uniqueness of the revelation of God in Jesus Christ.

The wise men saw the star 'as it rose'. They were on a journey of faith. The science of astrology is one thing. The act of faith, kneeling before the Christ Child is quite another. The popular perception of the Christmas story is one of simplicity. The simple shepherds were the first to recognise Jesus. 'Christmas is for children', we say. But the Archbishop of Canterbury tells us that 'the story of Christmas reminds us that coming to the Christ Child isn't always simple. People come by roundabout routes with complex histories, sin and muddle, false perceptions and wrong starts. It's no good saying to them, and us, 'you must become simple and wholehearted'. The real question is, 'Can you take all your complicated history with you on a journey towards the manger?'

He goes on to say, 'Don't deny the tangle and the talents, the varied web of what has made you who you are. Every step is part of the journey. Even the false starts are part of the journey, experience that moves you towards the truth. It won't do to think of Christianity as a faith that demands an embarrassed pretence of a simplicity that has no connection with reality.'

It is only when the gospel writers recognise Jesus as the Christ, hanging on the wood of the cross on a hill outside Jerusalem, that they can look back thirty-three years and gaze down to Bethlehem and see the suffering servant, the saviour of the world lying in the wood of the crib. This is true not only of the gospel writers. Our lives, too, are suspended between the wood of the cross and the wood of the crib. Where is God in the midst of the complex of human existence? 'Here', says Jesus, with arms outstretched on the wood of birth and death.

When the wise men discovered Jesus they opened their treasures. When we are touched by the same Lord we are compelled to offer the treasure of our lives. For the new priest that treasure contains his faith, his love, his dedication to God. His treasure means bringing his legal and academic skills, his historical and, dare I say, even political skills to the service of God's people and God's Church.

All this is summed up surely in the final poignant sentence of the Epiphany story. 'They were warned in a dream not to go back to Herod *but returned to their own country by a different way*.' Once you have experienced the vision of Jesus, once you experience the fullness of his presence in his Church, in the sacraments, through his people, once you have been ordained for service, you travel like the wise men 'by a different route'. You have chosen that new route, Mark, and must now be a sign for others on their journey. Rowan Williams again, 'Bring what has made who you are and bring it neither in pride nor in embarrassment, but in order to offer it as gift.' Thank you for the gift of your life to the priesthood. Just as you will soon change the gifts of bread and wine into the body and blood of Jesus, you too will be changed into 'another Christ' for the glory of God and the well-being of his people.

Can the last word go to Christina Rossetti and my favourite carol?

> What can I offer, poor though I am.
> If I were a shepherd, I would bring a lamb.
> If I were a wise man, I would do my part.
> What can I offer? I will give my heart.

In the end, all that we have to offer is the fullness of our heart with all that signifies personally and spiritually. It is with a full heart that you move now to celebrate the mystery of faith in which we experience the revelation of God in communion with his only Son, Jesus Christ.

Augustinian Recollects Twenty-fifth Anniversary at Kensal New Town 8 February 2003

First Reading: Job 7:1–4, 6–7
Second Reading: 1 Corinthians 9:16–19, 22–23
Gospel: Mark 1:29–39

Looking back, twenty-five years seems a very short time. 'Where has the time gone?' we say. 'It seems like only yesterday.' Looking forward, however, twenty-five years seems an extraordinarily long period of time. We can hardly plan for next year. We often say, 'who knows what the future will bring?' It is particularly relevant, of course, at this time of international tension.

Believe it or not, our reading from the Book of Job casts light even on our celebration today. Six hundred years before the time of Jesus, Job is tried and tested. He loses everything and suffers greatly. But at the heart of his suffering lies the restlessness which is at the heart of the human condition. Listen again to what he says:

> Lying in bed, I wonder when will it be day. Risen, I think, how slowly evening comes. Restlessly, I fret till twilight falls.

The words of St Augustine are a help to all of us in the midst of our turmoil. He prayed: 'Thou hast made us for thyself, O Lord, and our hearts shall find no rest until they rest in thee.'

The sons of St Augustine who have served this parish since 1978 have provided 'a still point in a turning world'.

(T.S. Elliot) And the physical church building is over a hundred years old. As the area here was demolished and new buildings put up all around, this church has remained as a sign of the permanent presence of God, a call to worship, a call to service.

But the Church is not just a building, not just bricks and mortar. The Church is the people who believe, who worship, who build up the Body of Christ, who serve their local community. This 'living Church' has been nurtured and educated by an outstanding school, which still breathes the charism of Catherine McCauley and the Sisters of Mercy. That 'living Church' has been nourished and sustained first by the extraordinary vision of Cardinal Manning and his Oblates of St Charles; then by our own diocesan priests; and, for the last twenty-five years, by the Augustinian Recollects. Even I remember the welcoming smile of Fr Dennis Caddle and Fr John Curry when I came here with a son of Kensal New Town, one of four priests ordained from here, Fr Dermot Power.

I know the struggles that priests and people of the '70s had as they tried and succeeded in securing the fabric so that this church was not closed down. Once secure, Fr Patrick O'Haven was able to consolidate and beautify this building and make it what it is today. The Diocese is grateful to Fr Frank Umendia and Fr Hugh Corrigan, together with that honorary Augustinian, Sr Margarita Cunningham, for the dedication and service that they offer to the people of this parish.

I am sure that they and their predecessors will echo the words of St Paul to the problematic Christian community in Corinth:

> Do you know what my reward is? It is this. That in my preaching to be able to offer the good news free, and not insist on the rights which the gospel gives me.

And in that preaching, the parish puts into practice the example of Jesus in tonight's Gospel extract. The parish cares for those who are suffering from diseases of one sort or another. It casts out the devils of ignorance, prejudice, fear, racism. Being Recollects, these Augustinian Fathers seek to bring people apart to a separate place in order to teach them to pray. In the celebration of Mass and Holy Communion, it gives us food for the journey so that like Jesus we may go to neighbouring places to preach there too, because that is why Jesus came and that is what we are called to do. The Church is missionary and needs to look beyond itself in order to make itself whole.

As we celebrate twenty-five years of service by the Augustinian Recollects in this parish, we could do no better than repeat the prayer of today's Mass:

> In faith and love we ask you Father to watch over your family gathered here. In your mercy and loving kindness no thought of ours is left unguarded, no tear unheeded, no joy unnoticed. Through the prayer of Jesus may the blessings promised to the poor in spirit lead us to the treasures of your heavenly kingdom. Amen.

Kieran Murtagh, SSCC
Ordination to the Priesthood
20 June 2003

This is the third ordination I have attended at Our Lady of Lourdes in Acton. The first was on 20 May 1972, the day before I was ordained a priest. The second was 1991, a very hot summer's day. I still remember the rhythm of the drumbeats coming from the market opposite. Little did I suspect that at the third ordination I would be sitting here on the other side of the proceedings. It's just one reminder to me, and I suspect Kieran as well, that the Lord does work in mysterious ways. We do believe in a God of Surprises. God does have plans for us which are quite different to our own, and our task is to listen in faith and respond to his invitation whether it comes from the Holy Father, or from the Congregation of the Sacred Hearts, to serve God and his people in his way and not in ours. Those called in unexpected ways to service in new circumstances have to respond to God's call like Jeremiah: 'Do not say: I do not know how to speak... Go now to those to whom I send you ... Do not be afraid, for I am with you to protect you.' (Jer. 1:4–9)

Total availability to the service of the Gospel is surely at the heart of the missionary vocation, and the charism of the Sacred Heart Fathers. 'Our consecration calls us to the dynamism of saving love and fills us with zeal for our mission.' That must be a reflection of the gift of self which is symbolised by the Sacred Heart of Jesus who offers himself in sacrificial love. The link between his love for us portrayed on the cross of Calvary is the Eucharist which we celebrate today and every day in the life of the Church. At this ordination of a new priest whose life will be defined by the Eucharist, may I reflect with you on the Pope's recent letter about the Church and the Eucharist. The Pope writes:

> ... the People of the New Covenant ... become a 'sacrament' for humanity, a sign and instrument of the salvation achieved by Christ ... for the redemption of all. The Church's mission stands in continuity with the mission of Christ: 'As the Father sent me, so am I sending you.'
> (*Ecclesia de Eucharistia*, 22)

In other words, when members of the Church come together to celebrate the Eucharist we are meant to be a sign of that unity, that Holy Communion, that Civilisation of Love spoken of by Pope Paul VI, which is the foundation of harmony in society at large.

If we as a people are called to be that sign of communion, so too is the priest meant to be a unifier, a reconciler, a servant. According to the Pope's letter,

> the priest is called to be 'in persona Christi'. By that he isn't acting just 'in the name of Christ' or 'in place of Christ'. 'In persona' means a specific sacramental identification with the High Priest in this sacrifice in which, in truth, nobody can take His place. In celebrating the Eucharist the priest transforms the ordinary efforts of people to worship God, and links the Eucharistic consecration to the Sacrifice of the Cross and the Last Supper. (*Ecclesia de Eucharistia*, 29)

Kieran, like all the priests here today, will be aware of that high calling, but will also echo the words of the reading from the Letter to the Hebrews: 'He can deal gently with the ignorant and the wayward, since he himself is beset with weakness. Because of this he is bound to offer sacrifice for his own sins as well as for those of the people'.

As a member of the Congregation of the Sacred Hearts, our new priest cannot, and does not, do this alone. The strength of the religious life, and the fruitfulness of his priesthood, will be a reflection of the charism of the community to which he has given his life. 'The congregation lives out its mission in an international, collaborative and family minded spirit, nourished by the Eucharist . . . We believe that adoration and contemplation situate us in the presence of God's saving love, and help us discern the signs of the times in which we live, so that with Christ, we may restore our world through the total gift of ourselves.'

The prayer and action of this ordination express those truths in a language beyond any merely human words. Kieran will prostrate himself before the altar. A sign of abandonment to the will of God, a sign of humility and unworthiness in the presence of God. A sign of trust in the power of God. The Bishop 'lays hands' on his head, a handing on of power, of authority to act in the name of the Church and of Christ. Once more, the Pope says in his letter on the Eucharist: 'This priest is a gift which the assembly receives through Episcopal succession rooted in the Apostles'. He is clothed in vestments to remind him, and us, he is not acting as an individual in leading worship and in serving God's people. Those vestments clothe us in Christ, wrap us in his love and his dignity as, despite our personal inadequacies, we make Christ present in His way, not in ours. His hands are anointed with the oil of chrism, the oil of Christ, Christ the servant, Christ the King. That anointing reminds the new priest he is to handle sacred things. He has to make people holy by his hands lifted up in prayer. And then he receives the gifts of the people to be offered to God. And the words used by the Bishop are a reminder to him, and to us, that the vocation we follow has to be renewed and relived, celebrated and proclaimed every day of our lives:

> Know what you are doing. Imitate the mystery you celebrate. Model your life on the mystery of the Lord's cross.

Fr Richard Andrew Induction as Parish Priest St George's, Enfield Exaltation of the Holy Cross 13 September 2003

In the year 381 an extraordinary woman called Egeria set off from Spain on an epic journey to the Holy Places in Palestine and Egypt. She kept a diary of her three-year pilgrimage. The diary is one of the most vibrant and illuminating accounts of the social, political and religious landscape of the Mediterranean world in the fourth century. Egeria went to Jerusalem in the footsteps of another amazing woman, Helena, the mother of the Emperor Constantine.

Helena had gone to Jerusalem on pilgrimage in the year 280. In a great archaeological and spiritual adventure, she discovered that the hill of Calvary had been built on by the Roman occupying forces. Instead of a church on the Holy Sepulchre she found a Pagan Temple. Jerusalem had its political, security and religious problems long before the Intifada of our own time.

Helena in the third century and Egeria in the fourth developed the devotions we now call 'creeping to the Cross', 'Stations of the Cross' and our Good Friday liturgy. The need people felt to see and touch sacred relics, the desire to kiss the wood of the cross, was obviously a climax of all this devotion. But lest our mayor and members of parliament, our police and community workers think that vandalism and crime are a product of 21st-century Britain, let me read from

Egeria's pilgrim diary about what went on in Jerusalem on Good Friday:

> Now the Bishop holds the sacred wood firmly in his hands. He is guarded by deacons because when the people come to kiss it, I have been told that sometimes they bite off and steal pieces of the sacred wood. It is thus guarded by the deacons who stand around, lest anyone approaching should do so again.

Unravelling all that history and devotion we come to today's feast in the Church calendar: the Exaltation of the Holy Cross. We Christians are convinced that the Cross stands at the crossroads of the human story. The lowest point of human history becomes the highest point of God's revelation. At a particular point in history, God reveals himself in Jesus Christ. Jesus challenges the social order, traditional religious practice, accepted moral norms, and because of this, is rejected. Get rid of the messenger and we don't have to listen to the message. Where is God in the midst of persecution of the innocents, in the midst of human suffering, in the midst of degrading death? 'Here', says Jesus, with arms outstretched on the Cross. Hanging on the Cross, Jesus does not withdraw God's love. Does not say they don't deserve what I have done for them. In the midst of suffering, Jesus goes on revealing, goes on loving, goes on forgiving. 'Father forgive them, they know not what they do.' His sacrifice is the key to our faith that evil will never triumph over good. Our belief that no suffering is wasted in the sight of God.

So we erect a cross in our churches, schools and homes. We wear a cross around our necks. We carry a cross in our own lives. We identify with that world-changing event which binds our struggle with that of Jesus' confrontation with suffering, pain, sin, death and evil, and we do it in the light of our personal faith in his resurrection, we do it in the historic faith and tradition of the Church, we do it inspired by the faith practised in our church communities.

It is the duty of the priest to re-present (to represent) all that in word and sacrament and in service in this time and in this place to these people. This is one reason we surround the appointment of a new pastor with such ceremony. He is given the keys to the church. Not just that he is the caretaker or the maintenance man for St George's. Keys signify the authority of service to this community. He is given the Book of the Gospels from which he will preach so that the printed words may become the LIVING WORD as together we discover the lessons of life which conform to and reflect God's creative plan.

He is taken to the place of Baptism where the water reminds us of the life Jesus gives us not just for the seventy or eighty years we live on earth but for that union with God which is eternal life. He is sat down not just in any chair, but in the President's chair where he will be seen as the head of the Body of Christ, the people from every background and walk of life who are bonded together in faith and love. Finally he will be given the bread and wine to be offered at Mass, obeying the command of Jesus to re-member, to put back together again the broken members of his sacrifice on Calvary.

If you think that is an impossible job description for any priest, you are absolutely right. It only becomes remotely possible by his life of faith and prayer. It is made more possible by the extraordinary vitality, giftedness, goodwill and dedication of the people in St George's parish and the 220 parishes of this Diocese of Westminster. We are committed not just to building up and sustaining our own Catholic life but to being of service to the wider community, in this case of Enfield. The presence of Ministers of other churches is a testimony to the tradition of ecumenical cooperation of all the churches here. The presence of representatives from our public life and service is a reassurance that in partnership the Catholic community of Enfield is at one with all who work in this borough for the creation of that 'civilisation of love' which is the core of all democracy and multi-cultural society.

And I speak from personal experience when I say that in your new parish priest, Fr Richard Andrew, you have a man of prayer and dedication, a man of courage and conviction, a man of humour and humility who will do great things for you and with you – and will inspire you to do great things in return.

Mill Hill College
Diaconate Ordination
13 December 2003

First Reading: Acts 8:26–39
Second Reading: Romans 12:3–19
Gospel: Mark 1:14–20

In February 1582, Pope Gregory XIII declared that the Julian Calendar would no longer be followed by Christian people. The change to the Gregorian calendar would take place on 4 October that year. One consequence of the change was that ten days would be lost. The day following the 4th was to be the 15th of October. The Protestants of Northern Europe thought this was a popish plot to deprive them of ten days of their lives. They refused to make the change. It was only in 1752 that the British Government accepted the inevitable and adopted the Gregorian calendar. That year the 2nd of September was followed the next day by the 14th of September.

According to the old Julian calendar, 13 December was the shortest day, the day of the winter solstice. The sun was at its lowest point in the sky. It was the darkest day of the year. No wonder our fathers in faith surrounded this feast with light and hope. What better feast to celebrate than the martyrdom of Lucy, named after the light. Her name and her witness in 304 to the truth of the Gospel must surely be an inspiration to those being ordained today. They will commit themselves to living and preaching and witnessing to that same Gospel in which Lucy lived and for which she died.

The deacon is commissioned, ordered, ordained to

preach that Gospel. The Bishop hands him the book of the Gospel in a formal way and with a powerful instruction. 'Receive the Gospel of Christ, whose herald you now are. Believe what you read. Teach what you believe. Practice what you teach.' He will know that the preaching of the word takes place not just in the pulpit, but in his life and in his heart. You will have to instruct and explain, accompanying people in their discernment and understanding of what God is saying in this place, at this time and in these circumstances. What a model for evangelisation you have in that extract from the Acts of the Apostles. Philip sat down by the side of the Ethiopian. He entered into his experience. He explained the scriptures to him. He elicited faith. A model for a missionary, inculturisation, interfaith dialogue, exploration of the things of faith.

The Deacon is called to be Faith-full. Paul put it well in his letter to the Romans, 'Do not give up when trials come'. The questions before the ordination are a reminder that every day you have to renew that commitment in order to be Christ to others. Will you hold the mystery of faith with a clear conscience? Will you maintain and deepen a spirit of prayer? Will you shape your life according to the Gospel? Do you possess yourself as completely as you can so that you can make a free gift of your human right to intimacy, love, marriage, parenthood, in the gift of celibacy? 'I will, I do, I am, with the help of God.'

The ordination reminds us, and yourselves, that no matter what your gifts of preaching, teaching, administration, prophecy, you need to be open to receive the greatest gift of all – the gift of the grace offered by Jesus Christ. As a sign of that willingness to be filled with Christ you prostrate yourself before the altar in prayer. That is a gesture of emptiness and humility. It is a gesture of abandonment and trust. It is a sign of your willingness to be filled with the power and love of God – not just for yourselves, but for the good of those you serve.

The word-less power of the Sacrament is expressed in the Laying on of Hands. That gesture links you directly to the handing on of the tradition which will be your task from today. That action is supported by the extraordinarily beautiful words in the prayer of ordination:

> May they remain strong and steadfast in Christ
> Giving to the world a witness of a true conscience.

Isn't that what 'being ready for the Kingdom' in today's Gospel is about. 'Your word is a lamp for my steps and a light for my ways.' But not just a light for your own journey of faith. You must be prepared to guide, direct and support others in their search and discovery of truth. You will need to be the Philip not just to Ethiopians, but to the people of all countries in Africa, and Asia, and beyond. You need to be light and shining on the Kingdom. You will need to use all your gifts for the glory of God and the well-being of his people. That is why we pray on this, your ordination day.

May God who has begun the good work in you bring it to fulfilment.

Eulogy for Bishop Victor Guazzelli, Well-known and loved Auxiliary Bishop of Westminster

Born London - 19 March 1920
Died - 1 June 2004

The love affair between Victor Guazzelli and the country and people of Portugal began in 1935. In that year he travelled to Lisbon as a fifteen-year-old boy to begin studying for the priesthood at the English College. Founded in 1628, the College continued to educate students for the priesthood until its closure in 1970. In those pre-war years, it was not unusual for gifted boys to be sent abroad to study in this way. Guazzelli was well suited to the challenge of continental Catholicism as the son of Italian immigrants born in London's East End on 19 March 1920. His proud Italian father pointed out to the impressionable teenager that, as the only son, the family name would not be carried on were he ordained a priest. Nonetheless he gave the young Victor his blessing as he set off on his journey from Southampton early on a September morning.

The declaration of war in 1939 ensured that the separation from home and family lasted even longer than expected. Students and priests at the English College became exiles from their own country for over ten years. Not only had Guazzelli left England as a boy to return as a priest after the war, but his father had died in the meantime.

His natural urbanity and gift for languages made Victor ideal for his first appointment in London to the cosmopolitan parish of St Patrick, Soho Square, where he ministered from 1945 until 1948. He was recalled to Lisbon to teach Scripture and act as Bursar to the College for the next ten years. The first task was a privilege and a delight, giving him a lifelong love of Scripture and a gift for preaching. The second was not to his liking!

In 1958 he was appointed first as chaplain and then Sub-Administrator to the colourful Mgr Francis Bartlett at Westminster Cathedral. These were tumultuous years as the Church at large and the Cathedral in particular tried to digest the liturgical changes envisaged by the Second Vatican Council.

Appointed Parish Priest to St Thomas' Church in Fulham in 1968, he thrived on the joy of being a parish priest. Sadly, this was not to last too long as Cardinal Heenan, recognising the respect in which he was held, appointed him Vicar General of the Archdiocese of Westminster. In 1970 he was created an Auxiliary Bishop of the Diocese and was particularly proud of the Titular See of Lindisfarne to which he was appointed. He was even more proud and grateful when the membership committee of the Shooters Hill Golf Club recognised Lindisfarne as an off-shore island. It qualified him as an 'overseas' member and allowed him to indulge his lifelong passion for golf at a fee he could afford! He was grateful for his association with his local golf club which was literally a tunnel ride away from his beloved Poplar.

For almost thirty years he gave himself in unstinted service to the priests and people of the Diocese. When, in 1976, Cardinal Basil Hume created Pastoral Areas to be served by his Auxiliary Bishops, Victor Guazzelli was the natural choice to look after the London Boroughs of Camden, Islington, Hackney and Tower Hamlets. He thrived in these new responsibilities, identifying totally with the people of his birthplace. During the late '60s and throughout the '70s, when the East End of London was convulsed with industrial action at Wapping, the redevelopment of Canary Wharf and new tides of immigration, Guazzelli was able to speak with authority to workers, community leaders, and the London Docklands Development Corporation. His was the authority of one who lived amidst the people. He was not afraid to challenge the injustices they experienced as the traditional way of life was being changed at their expense. He used his influence to identify the structures of injustice using his voice for the voiceless. Recognising the need for a new style of ministry amongst priests emphasising 'mission' rather than 'maintenance', he gathered around himself a group of diocesan priests who would conduct six-weeks intensive missions and programmes of lay formation in parishes. Affectionately known as 'The God Squad' this experiment was visionary and challenging. He regarded it as one of the most fruitful times of his episcopate.

His passion for justice involved him in the work of Pax Christi whose President he became in 1975. This necessarily involved him in sometimes unpopular, often controversial, causes. His gentle, reassuring style ensured that disagreements did not result in conflict. His first-hand experience of the social and demographic changes taking place in the East End of London made him ideally qualified for the Inter-Faith dialogue which he pursued seriously. This also made him the obvious choice as Chairman of the Bishops' Committee for Faith and Cultures. Pax Christi paid tribute to his easy rapport in international groups and his moral courage on the subject of war and disarmament:

> We have appreciated his willingness to do the right thing and to 'stick his neck out' when necessary . . . he identified with ordinary people . . . and attempted to make justice a priority for the East London area.

In 1993, as the Bishops' representative on the Apostleship of the Sea, he took a leading role in reinvigorating and reconstructing this important outreach of the Church to seafarers throughout the world by means of a series of 'Port Chaplaincies'.

His Portuguese connection made him the ideal candidate to visit Bishop Bello in East Timor on two occasions, each at the height of the civil conflict between that fledgling democracy and Indonesia. Long before the injustices experienced by the people of East Timor were recognised by the West, Guazzelli was lobbying government and Church agencies on the human rights which were being violated there. In undertaking these visits he offered outstanding personal and pastoral support to the isolated and virtually unknown Bishop Bello. Guazzelli was gratified when the international community eventually recognised Bello's extraordinary work in defence of human rights with the award of the Nobel Prize.

As a member of the Latin American Desk of the Catholic Relief Agency CAFOD, he visited various programmes organised by CAFOD in Brazil during 1981 and demonstrated an enduring commitment to Latin America. He served for the last decade on CAFOD's Latin America Committee. At different times Cardinal Arns and Archbishop Helder Camara came to see him at his home in East London. Once more, his vision of Episcopal ministry extended far beyond his responsibilities in Westminster.

He will be remembered by generations of Lisbonians for the skilful way in which he negotiated with the government of Portugal over the closure of the English College in Lisbon and the maintenance of an English Catholic presence in that country. His passion for golf, shared by many of his fellow clergy, was indulged in the house he established in Faro both as a place of recreation and retreat for priests from all over England.

Three years after the normal age of retirement for Bishops, Victor Guazzelli left Pope John House in Poplar, and the community of the Faithful Companions of Jesus with whom he had worked and returned to Westminster Cathedral as an honorary chaplain. For almost five years he made an outstanding contribution to the life and ministry of the Cathedral, taking his place on the rota of Masses and Confessions, a willing listener to the many people who came to seek advice, and a great example of dedicated and cheerful service to his fellow clergy.

His obvious compassion and availability to the sick and the vulnerable was evident in the outstanding commitment he made to the Handicapped Children's Pilgrimage Trust. This organisation has taken 2,000 sick and disabled children to Lourdes after Easter for over twenty-five years. Victor was the stable episcopal presence throughout much of that time.

Amidst all his gifts and achievements, Victor Guazzelli will be remembered most as a 'People's Bishop'. He was also recognised as a Bishop who had extraordinary compassion for priests. His life was based on Gospel values which expressed themselves in dedication, courage, optimism and prayer.

Nightingale Fellowship Service
St Thomas' Hospital
14 May 2005

Gospel: Luke 8:41–56

I was delighted to read in the introduction to this service that Mary Seacole was to be remembered also. Two hundred years after her birth, it is good to pay tribute to this pioneering woman, this nurse, this heroine of the Crimean War. With her Jamaican background, and the slave conditions she endured, she has become a role model for the liberation of those who are oppressed, a voice for the voiceless, the Maya Angelou of her own day. As we celebrate the heritage of Florence Nightingale today, and the Training School named after her, it is good to pay tribute to the nurses and doctors from the Caribbean who have made such a contribution to medical care in this country.

Today's service takes place in the Anglican and Catholic Dioceses of Southwark. So it is fitting also to pay tribute to the Sisters of Mercy from Bermondsey who responded to the invitation of Bishop Thomas Grant to send nurses to join Florence Nightingale in 1854. Sr Mary Clare Moore was one of fifteen Irish nuns who nursed with her in the Crimean. The role of nursing sisters (of the religious variety) needs to be acknowledged not just in church-run hospitals, but in the Hospices and Nursing Homes of our own day as well.

We seem to be surrounded by women! Even today's Gospel passage is focussed on women. The woman who had been suffering from a haemorrhage for twelve years was not only distressed by her medical condition. She was oppressed by the social constraints of her condition as well. According to Jewish law, she was 'ritually unclean'. Everything with which she came into contact was 'unclean'. To touch was taboo. So her courage and desperation in 'touching even his cloak' was radical indeed.

This incident teaches us something about the cost of healing. 'Who touched me?' That engagement took something from him. He felt power going out of him. At the end of an exhausting day of nursing, diagnosing, teaching, dispensing, administering, comforting, those who care in this profession must surely feel 'power going out of them'. The human face of compassion and professionalism is the price we pay for service.

The Gospel scene tells us something about the disciples. Theirs is a commonsense approach. How could he avoid being touched. He was in the middle of a crowd being jostled and pushed. So how could he ask 'Who touched me'? I am reminded of the words of our late Pope, John Paul II. He said,

> I don't like the word 'crowd' which seems to be anonymous. I prefer the word 'multitude'. My own office causes me to meet many people, sometimes great multitudes. I have never felt I was meeting an excessive group of people. Each person is unique, and I was anxious to preserve the personal contact of each relationship.

For that woman, this was a unique and significant encounter. For the hundreds of patients and staff that encounter their own nurse, you are the human face of the medical profession.

The encounter tells us something about the woman herself. She was covert. Hidden in the crowd. Afraid to ask because of her isolation and desperation. She fell at his feet and told him the whole truth. It takes time and patience to listen, to elicit from people their hopes and fears, their joys and aspirations. Her confession becomes a source of peace and healing for her. Confessions don't only take place in churches and are not just heard by priests. You will know of the secrets of people's hearts which are entrusted to those who care for them at the most vulnerable periods of their lives.

And there is another woman, at the threshold of adulthood who demands our attention. She is twelve years old. She has lived exactly the same time as the woman had been burdened by her illness. She is to be given back her life as well. But first Jesus must separate the external confusion from the inner reality. He removes distractions and focuses attention. 'Why all this commotion and wailing. The child is not dead but asleep. They laughed at him. So he turned them all out.' The scene could be reminiscent of Accident and Emergency in our city hospitals on a Saturday night!

As your colleagues have to turn to vulnerable adolescents, teenage girls, and deal with health issues, medical ethics, confidentiality, the rights of parents, the duty of care, you have to weigh the sometimes conflicting values of morality and law, of the rights of the individual and the implications for society. They have to repeat those words of Jesus not just to the onlookers but to the patient herself. You have to say, 'She is not dead but only asleep.' She needs to awake to new life, fulfilled life, health education, mature relationships.

It is no accident that when Pope John Paul came to England he celebrated the Anointing of the Sick not one mile from here at St George's Southwark. All through his life he preached the dignity of the human person, from the womb to the tomb. He proclaimed that the sick and vulnerable have much to teach us about the value of human life. His final illness gave him the opportunity to express his belief in God even in the midst of suffering and pain. He was unequivocal in his admiration, support and prayer for those who care for the sick and invest them, us, with dignity at every stage of their illness.

So during this annual Nightingale Fellowship Service, let us pray for the sick who depend on the skill and dedication of nurses and doctors for their physical, spiritual and emotional well-being. Let us pray for all members of the medical profession that they might continue to be inspired by the highest ideals and sustained in their healing work. Let us pray for those who have died that they may experience the vision of God who created them and calls them to himself. And let us pray for each other that each one will continue to be a source of strength and support for the others.

Amen.

Neville Dyckhoff
Diaconate Ordination
25 June 2006

First Reading: Job 38:1, 8–11
Second Reading: 2 Corinthians 5:14–17
Gospel: Mark 4:35–41

In the year 1913, the famous Swiss psychologist Carl Jung parted company with his equally famous colleague, Sigmund Freud. Two different approaches to analytical psychology and the treatment of psychiatric illnesses resulted. Freudian and Jungian analysis still define different ways of dealing with psychological problems today.

Jung explored what he called 'the collective unconscious'. He developed what is called 'dream analysis'. He wrote about five great 'archetypes' which define our thoughts and patterns of behaviour. One of these archetypal dreams was of a calm sea with a ship sailing through it, pointing at a lighthouse. The surface of life. But beneath the surface the water is teeming with turmoil. The dark, the deep, the unknown, the repressed, the subconscious. All represented by the sea. And, when analysed, expressing suffering, pain, destructive urges, feelings of personal failure. On a wider stage, innocent suffering, unjust persecution, the absence of God. The sea is as potent a physical force as it is a spiritual one, as we saw in the Tsunami disaster just over a year ago.

When the good man Job suffered in the Old Testament, he asked the same questions that we ask today: Why does God allow this to happen? Where is God in the midst of human pain? Why do the innocent suffer? Job wept and raged at God. He was in despair and anguish as he questioned God. But his faith triumphed not least as a result of the answer God gave in today's first reading:

> Who pent up the sea behind closed doors?
> Who marked the bounds it was not to cross?
> Who said, 'Come no further. Your proud waves shall break.'

Carl Jung would have approved of that!

Today's gospel passage doesn't just describe a storm on the Sea of Galilee. The early Church experienced the storm of persecution and martyrdom. Those who read it would be personally familiar with the struggle individuals had to keep faith in Jesus in the midst of crisis, confusion and fear. So the prayer of crisis and panic would have been on the lips of innocent suffers as on those of the disciples in the boat. 'Lord, don't you care? Can't you intervene and do something? We don't deserve to die for following our consciences and doing good in following you.' And Jesus says to them, and to us, 'Where is your faith?' And to the sea, and to the turmoil that lies beneath, he says. 'Be quiet. Be calm. Have faith.'

On the sea of dreams, Carl Jung describes a lighthouse. We say Jesus is our light in the midst of darkness and of the storm. I hope it isn't too much to say that the one called to Diaconal ministry in the Church is called to be a light and a guide to others too. He is ordained, ordered, focussed on Jesus who is the Way, the Truth and the Life. The ministry of the Deacon focuses and makes present the power of Jesus in the midst of the circumstances of everyday life. In the joys and hopes, the sufferings and the sadness of the people he serves, the consistency and calm, his availability and unchanging dedication is a still point in a turning world.

The Deacon needs to hear the Word of God in the storm, as Job did. He needs to be able to explain it and to live it in order to be a preacher of that word. There's more to preaching than standing in a pulpit – or even sitting in a chair. To bear one another's burdens. This is the ministry of service. 'Be calm. Have faith. I am with you.'

Everything we do in this ceremony of ordination expresses a different facet of these truths. The questions on prayer, on authentic preaching, on availability in service, on obedience. To listen to the bishop 'with an attentive ear.' And the answer: 'I am, with the help of God.'

The invocation of saints reminds us that although his ministry is rooted in this time and place and in a particular situation, it is not limited by history. It has an eternal dimension, linked to those who have gone before us marked with the Sign of Faith.

The Laying on of Hands is that ancient Apostolic gesture which links us with the early Church, links us with the disciples in the boat, recognises that, though the storms and turmoil we face on the seas of the twenty-first century might be different to our fathers in faith, we still face Jesus with wonder and awe. 'Who can this be? Even the wind and the sea obey him.'

The clothing with Diaconal vestments reminds Neville that he is not alone. Membership of the order of Deacons tells us we are not performing a personal function made up of our own insights, depending on our own resources, purveying our own opinions. This is a ministry 'of the Church' which will be focussed and expressed in what you do and in who you are, but is greater than any one of us who are called to minister. The vestments we wear cover up our personal idiosyncrasies and inadequacies. They remind us that 'we carry this treasure in earthen vessels.'

The comfort and the challenge of the Gospel is expressed in the handing on of the Book of the Gospels. The Deacon is told:

> Believe what you read.
> Teach what you believe
> And practice what you teach.

The new Deacon will no doubt reflect on the words of Paul to the Christians at Corinth: 'For anyone who is in Christ there is a new creation.' As a Deacon, Neville, you will be 'in Christ' in new and different ways. At the beginning of this 'new way' you will know that there will be much to give and much to receive. You will be comforted in the words of another prayer in the rite of ordination:

May God who has begun the good work in you bring it to perfection. Amen.

An Address Given to the Permanent Deacons, Leeds 23 November 2006

In the July 2006 issue of the *Pastoral Review,* there was a beautiful article by Bishop Michael Evans called 'The Deacon: An Icon of Christ the Servant'. I am sure many of you read it. In the article, Bishop Michael places service, the ministry of charity, the outreach to the poor and marginalized, as the prime function of the restored Diaconate. Of course he also speaks about the Deacon as a minister of Word and Sacrament, and collaborating with the bishop and priest in the ordained ministry. But the servant model is the primary one to be kept in view. Once I had read that article, I thought I had my talk prepared for you today!

Imagine my surprise when I read my copy of the *Pastoral Review* for November 2006. Another excellent article on the Diaconate, this time by Anthony Golley. It is called 'Deacons and the Servant Myth'. In his article he peels away the linguistic and functional layers of paint on the icon of Christ and explores what is really meant in Acts chapter 6 verses 1 – 7. This is what he says:

> The Greek-speaking Christians are complaining that their widows are being neglected in the daily *diakonia*. In Acts, the *diakonia* is the proclamation of the gospel (J. N. Collins, *Deacons and the Church*, p. 52). They are neglected for two reasons. First, the Aramaic-speaking Apostles predominantly concentrate their proclamation in the Temple area. The widows, who cannot comprehend the language and who for social reasons are most restricted in the home, are overlooked in this daily *diakonia*. The solution proposed by the

> Apostles, and agreed by the whole Church, is to appoint seven from among the Greek-speaking community to do this daily *diakonia* in the homes of the Greek widows or, as the expression in Greek has it, 'to minister at tables'.

In other words, as I understand it, the *diakonia* has a religious, liturgical and catechetical function, not to be confused with the ordinary meaning of servers of food and drink. J. N. Collins explores the Church Fathers in this area, not least St Ignatius in his *Letter to the Trallians*. Ignatius writes: 'Deacons are not waiters (*diakoni*) providing food and drink but executives (*hyperetai*) of the Church of God.'

Anthony Golley traces the origins of the functional diaconate, if I can put it like that, more to the Reformed Lutheran churches of Northern Europe. I've read elsewhere that the deacon in that reformed tradition has come to be seen as a kind of ordained social worker, carrying out the caring apostolate of the Church, rather like our SVP, or shelter for the homeless like the Passage, or the work of the Catholic Children's Society. It was that kind of model that prevented Cardinal Hume from embracing the restored Diaconate in the Diocese of Westminster. He felt it might undermine the role of the laity, or help them to abdicate their responsibility flowing from the common priesthood of all the baptised.

Of course the Michael Evans approach to Diaconate and that of Anthony Golley are not mutually exclusive. But they do help us peel away the different layers and understand the different strands which have contributed to your reflection recently, 'The deacon as the icon of Christ'. And when I say 'strip away the layers', I don't just mean that an icon is a picture glued onto wood and painted over with gold and contained in a silver frame. The creator of an icon approaches the work as an invitation to prayer, entering into a relationship with the subject, engaging in a spiritual relationship with the one who is to be honoured and venerated in this holy object. Western art looks for a realistic presentation, asks you to look at the subject from the outside in, tries to create a true likeness. Eastern art invites us to look outwards from within. It invites us to engage with the qualities of the object, with the eyes of Jesus which can pierce the soul, the hand of authority, the bestowal of forgiveness. All portrayed in symbolic ways. The purpose of the icon is to bring together the outer and inner world so that in the sacred place of encounter we may embrace God.

The Archbishop of Canterbury [Rowan Williams] puts this well in his book *Praying with Icons*:

> Icons are never portraits, attempts to give you an accurate representation of some human situation or some human face that you cannot see. They are — like all our efforts in Christian living — human actions that seek to be open to God's action. It sounds a bit strange to call a picture an 'action' in this way; but creating an icon is, after all, something 'performed' in a fixed way, with the proper preparation of fasting and prayers, in the hope not that you will produce a striking visual image but that your work will open a gateway for God. Just as God works through the human person or event, you are painting, you are responding prayerfully to the action of God and allowing that action to continue in your life.

Not all of us are painters in the narrow sense. But each of us is God's work of art and we do create a picture of the world and our place in it in relation to God. I love one of the Collects at Mass which says, 'Help us to judge wisely the things of earth and measure them by the things of Heaven.' None of us can do that alone. In response to the revelation of God in the person of Jesus Christ we are bound together through faith and baptism into the Body of

Christ, which is the Church. That description of the Church in the Second Vatican Council as one 'divine and human interlocked reality' sums it all up for me. The human face of the Church will always be weak and vulnerable. But it is the task of the members of the Church to portray the face of Christ in their life and in their worship. Just as the Church is described as having those two elements of divine and human, so the bond between the lay and ordained is described in communion, in relationship as well.

The decree of the Second Vatican Council on the Church called *Lumen Gentium* reflected on the dignity and the role of the lay faithful and that of the ordained ministry in a very powerful way. In chapters 3 and 4, it discussed the common priesthood of the laity and the priesthood of the ordained ministry. In what I am going to say I am not just speaking of the priesthood of the presbyter (if that's not tautologous) but the priesthood which is shared by all those who are in a hierarchical relationship with the people.

The Vatican Council says the common priesthood of the laity and the ordained priesthood of the hierarchy differ in *essence* and not just in *degree*. Those who practice ordained ministry are not just representatives, or spokespersons, for the community. Unhelpfully, the Council does not articulate what the essential differences are. We have to turn to the *Catechism of the Catholic Church* to explore that. This is what it says in section 1547:

> While the common priesthood of the faithful is exercised by the unfolding of the baptismal grace – a life of faith, hope and charity, a life according to the Spirit; the ministerial priesthood is at the service of the common priesthood. It is directed at the unfolding of the baptismal grace of all Christians. The ministerial priesthood is a means by which Christ unceasingly builds up and leads his Church. For this reason

> it is transmitted by its own sacrament: the sacrament of Holy Orders.

This was expressed clearly and beautifully by John McDaid, the Principal of Heythrop, when he spoke to our diocese on the subject of Communion and Mission recently. I hope you don't mind my reading his two key paragraphs:

> . . . it is thanks to the exercise of ministerial priesthood that the dignity of the baptised can be fully expressed. Ministerial priesthood is necessary, in other words, if the baptised are to do what they are supposed to do. Equally ministerial priesthood only exists for the sake of the common priesthood. Ministerial priesthood expresses Christ's service of the baptised, and this service is so crucial to the life of the Church that it requires a distinct identity (sacrament) and structure (transmission). Ministerial priesthood takes its origin in a specific authorisation by Christ to the Twelve to minister to the community in his name and this represents one of the constitutive features of the life of the Church, willed by Christ to be a structured communication of his grace within the life of the Church.
>
> Ministerial priesthood, then, is not *produced* by the common priesthood, since the common priesthood is the participation of all in the self-offering of Christ. The common priesthood, in union with Christ, is directed towards God. Ministerial priesthood is an expression of Christ's service of his people, one of the life-giving ways in which Christ ministers to them. The common priesthood is the service of God in union with Christ. Through ministerial priesthood, Christ serves the baptised. If you like to use the images of upwards and downwards — always potentially misleading but perhaps occasionally helpful — then common priesthood moves upwards from human beings to God, whilst ministerial priesthood is a downward form of divine service of the people.

So what do I want to say at the end of this talk? It is that the ministry of *diakonia* is the proclamation of the Gospel that all are redeemed in Christ. Even when that truth is not known, or not accepted, not understood or not lived, the proclamation must go on. The Church, and the common priesthood of its people, celebrates that truth and tries to live by it, deepening its understanding in a life of prayer, discipleship and worship. I want to say that the inner and outer landscape in which even faithful members of the Church are living out these truths is changing. Today's proclamation of the Gospel seems to me to demand that people are given the tools to help them engage with truths in different ways in order to face the internal and external challenges which are presented to us continually. One such instrument in our own diocese has no doubt been the faith-sharing groups which were set up as part of the 'At Your Word, Lord' program. Where the faith-sharing groups have been established, there has no doubt been a deepening of understanding and a desire for pastoral involvement. Almost 30,000 people have been involved at a deep level of study, reflection, prayer and sharing of faith.

There is a great need and desire in our lay faithful for formation in the Faith, for information and instruction too. What better way for a Deacon to respond to this need except by *Diakonia*, the service at tables in the truest sense of those words. Sitting with people and nourishing them by exploring the Gospel together, translating it into the circumstances of their lives. These tables may be at home, in schools and in parishes. It is in these places, and many others, that the priesthood of all the baptized is exercised through faith sharing, and ministered in breaking open the word in season and out of season.

Fr James Duffy Fortieth Anniversary of Priestly Ordination 21 May 2007

Forty is a biblical number! We first hear it in the Book of Genesis when rain fell on the earth for forty days and forty nights and Noah built his ark. In the book of Exodus we read that the People of Israel wandered in the desert for forty years as they sought to settle in the Promised Land. And in the New Testament, Jesus fasted for forty days and was tempted as he discerned what his true mission should be. No wonder the Church has enshrined the forty days in the season of Lent. The number forty speaks to us of Faith, Challenge, Hope and faithfulness to the revelation of God.

In our secular world, a fortieth anniversary is described as a Ruby anniversary. The ruby is the oldest of all the precious stones. It is red and warm and vibrant. It's the colour of blood. It's the colour of martyrdom. It reminds us of the Holy Spirit whose coming we prepare for in this week between Ascension and Pentecost. Have I given you enough ideas to start thinking about the priesthood on this fortieth anniversary of Fr Jim Duffy's Ordination?

At the Ordination of a priest, many powerful words are spoken and symbolic gestures performed. But the final words of the Ordination rite always remain fixed in my mind, said by the Bishop when he hands the bread and wine to the newly ordained:

> Accept the gifts of the people to be offered to God. Be conscious of what you are doing. Be as holy as the actions

> you perform. Model your life after the mystery of the Lord's Cross.

You might say to me 'but isn't that what all Christians are called to do, to follow the way of Christ, to live up to his example, to take up our cross and follow him every day in what we say and do and how we live?' And this is true. In baptism we accept his death and resurrection as the interrelation of everything that happens to us in our lives on earth. In Baptism we become members of the Body of Christ, parts of him, and so are called a 'priestly people'. We believe that God reveals himself to us in and through Jesus not just by giving us information about himself, but by allowing us to enter into communion with him that we might share God's life which is love. 'The glory of God is humanity fully alive', said St Irenaeus.

Our faith and baptism empowers us to worship God not just in our way, but in his way, ultimately through the representation of the sacrifice of love that Jesus made on the cross. On the cross, Jesus did not say: 'I have wasted my time. These people do not deserve what I have done for them. They are unforgivable. I withdraw God's love from them.' On the cross, Jesus goes on revealing, goes on loving, goes on forgiving - to the point of death and beyond. No wonder we are called a royal priesthood, a holy nation, a people set apart.

The *Catechism of the Catholic Church* explains how the priesthood of the laity and the ordained priesthood are 'ordered to one another'. This is what it says:

> Whilst the common priesthood of the faithful is exercised by the unfolding of the baptismal grace — a life of faith, hope and charity, a life according to the Spirit — the ministerial priesthood is at the service of the common priesthood. It is directed at the unfolding of the baptismal grace of all Christians. The ministerial priesthood is a *means* by which Christ

> unceasingly builds up and leads his Church. For this reason it is transmitted by its own sacrament, the sacrament of Holy Orders. (*CCC*, 1547)

The ordained priesthood is not produced by common priesthood, since common priesthood is the participation of us all in the participation of the self-offering of Christ. We worship God in and through communion with Jesus. The common priesthood is directed towards God. The ministerial priesthood is an expression of Christ's service to his people enabling, empowering them to become what they are called to be. The common priesthood is the service of God in communion with Christ. Through the ministerial priesthood, Christ serves those who are baptised. To use a simple image: The common priesthood moves upwards from human beings to God. The ministerial priesthood is a downward form of divine service of the people, from above to below as it were.

The conclusion of this? The more priestly office is exercised, the more baptismal dignity is expressed, the more a priest acts in a priestly way with our people, the more the grace of baptism comes to fulfilment in them. When a priest celebrates Mass, he is enabling the members of the Body of Christ to be priestly and to immerse their lives in Christ's priestly work.

Alan Neville, Missionary of the Sacred Heart
Admission to the Clerical State
13 January 2008

First Reading: Isaiah 42:1–4, 6–7
Second Reading: Acts 10:34–38
Gospel: Matthew 3:13–17

'The Art of Renaissance Siena' is the name of a marvelous exhibition which concluded today at the National Gallery in London. It was composed of pictures, statues, portraits, altar pieces and other devotional items from the fifteenth century city-state of Siena where St Catherine, the great Doctor of the Church, was so influential. Her remains are venerated to this day in the only Gothic church in Rome, the magnificent Santa Maria Sopra Minerva.

My favourite part of the exhibition was the display of triptychs. These are devotional items, aids to prayer, made up of three panels which can be opened up to focus on a particular scene from the life of Christ, or a patron saint whose life is portrayed to inspire the viewer to follow the path of sanctity trod by that saint. The most important panel is, of course, the central one, which is the focus and the foundation of the other two that reflect on the mystery of faith.

A triptych provides a good description of the reading to which we listen on this feast of the Baptism of our Lord. In the centre is the gospel scene: John baptizes Jesus in the Jordan. By tradition, John is often remembered as the last prophet of the Old Testament. It is equally true that he is the first prophet of the New Testament: 'Behold the Lamb of God ...' (Jn 1:29) At the very beginning of his public ministry, Jesus links himself with all that has gone before in the preaching of John. Through his Baptism at the hands of John, Jesus shows that he is the fulfillment of all Old Testament expectation of the Messiah. The concluding words of our gospel passage confirm this fulfillment: 'This is my Son, the Beloved' (Mt 3:17), words from the second psalm. Words recognized by faithful Jews as a description of the longed for Messiah. 'In whom I am well pleased'. Words of the prophet Isaiah describing the Suffering Servant foretold by the prophet. These are the words used by Matthew in recognition that the Christ would suffer.

As a devout Jew, Jesus would have been familiar with the words of the prophet Isaiah in the left-hand panel of today's scripture readings. He would have listened to them in the synagogue, particularly since his bar mitzvah. He would have recited and reflected on them at home.

> Here is my servant whom I uphold.
> He does not shout or cry aloud.
> Faithfully he brings justice.
> He will open the eyes of the blind.
> He will free captives from prison.
> He will bring light to those in darkness. (Is 42)

Little wonder the hostile reaction to him when he read them in public and said, 'These words are being fulfilled today, even as you listen'.

But we must go to the right-hand panel of our readings to see what they mean. Following the resurrection of Jesus from the dead, Peter realizes the radical nature of salvation Jesus came to proclaim, not just in words but in sacrificial action. 'The truth I have now come to realise is that God does not have favourites, but that anybody of any nationality who fears God and does what is right is acceptable to him.' (Acts 10:34) The universal call to holiness is made possible by the universality of the atoning death and resurrection of Jesus Christ.

We have just finished celebrating the triptych of the Advent, Incarnation, the Revelation of God in the birth of Jesus his Son. At Easter we celebrate the triptych of the Paschal Mystery, the journey from death to life. And our lives are interwoven in this pattern as we are drawn into the mystery of the Life, Death and Resurrection of our Lord. We paint ourselves into the masterpiece that he has already created for us – knowing that we are of infinite value in the sight of God. Loved to the point of death – and beyond.

The one who is commissioned to proclaim these truths in the public reading of the word of God is like a 'poet in residence' bringing the printed and spoken words to life in the minds and hearts of his hearers. He does so, in the first instance, by conveying the truth that the word of God has captivated and transformed his own life to the degree that he is offering himself for public ministry not just as a job or as a function, but as one captivated by the living word '. . . which is alive and active and cuts like a two-edged sword'. (Heb 4:12) By 'Admission into the Clerical State' the candidate is not being set apart as someone better or more perfect than others who seek to embrace '. . . the word of God spoken in the words of men'. He is anxious to personify in word and action that he has been captivated by love, that he can do nothing other than live by that word to the glory of God and in the service of God's people. Like William Blake, he will say:

Unless the eye catch fire
The God will not be seen.
Unless the ear catch fire
The God will not be heard.
Unless the tongue catch fire
The God will not be named.
Unless the heart catch fire
The God will not be loved.
Unless the mind catch fire
The God will not be known.

Alan Neville, Missionary of the Sacred Heart Diaconate Ordination 27 June 2008

Earlier this week I was privileged to celebrate Confirmation at St Elizabeth's Home, in Much Hadham. Many of you will know that this is one of the leading schools and homes for the care of people with severe epilepsy, autism, and many other related conditions. The children and young people there have very special educational needs. The Confirmation ceremony was unpredictable and noisy. The youngsters certainly fulfilled the description of 'challenging behaviour'. Looking around the chapel, I was struck by the parents who were touching, holding, often restraining their strong, sometimes forceful, always vulnerable teenage children.

And I thought that, when these children were born, the news of their condition must have put a hole in the heart of the family. But my experience has been that instead of fear and anger and bitterness at having an 'abnormal' child, there has poured out a river of unselfish and inexplicable love. These parents love their children not *despite* their disabilities but *because* of them. They love them not in spite of the relatively short time they will be with them, but because these things make every moment, every experience, every achievement, more precious. Their love is both instructive and deliberate. Instructive in that it sometimes makes no sense at all. It may seem irrational. Where is the 'gain' in educating and loving a child who, according to the measure of this world, is a failure, or defective. Their love is also deliberate. Those parents, and the Sisters and staff who dedicate themselves to the care of those children, use all of their skill, their intelligence, their energy to secure the safety and happiness of each wounded child.

If human beings can show such unselfish love for each other, how much more true is it of God himself? In Jesus, we see the innermost life of God revealed to us and for us in order to show how we should love one another. The cost of that revelation took Jesus to rejection, suffering and death. 'Get rid of the messenger and we don't have to listen to the message' was the logic of the crucifixion. But on the Cross, Jesus does not withdraw God's love. He does not say, 'these people do not deserve what I have done for them. They are unforgivable.' On the Cross, Jesus goes on revealing, goes on loving, goes on forgiving. The lowest point of human history thereby becomes the highest point of God's revelation. 'Where is God in the midst of human suffering?' 'Here', says Jesus with arms outstretched on the Cross.

The missionaries who are dedicated to the Sacred Heart of Jesus embrace these truths. They take their biblical inspiration from the piercing of the side of Jesus by the spear of the Roman soldier. St John tells us that from the wounded heart of Jesus there poured blood and water – symbols of the life of the Church. The charism of their founder, Fr Chevalier, is based on the fact that the heart is shorthand language for that which is deepest within the life of a person, that which motivates, that which gives identity meaning and purpose. It is no accident that the Bible refers to 'the heart' no fewer than 1,100 times. The prophet Ezekiel puts it well when he says, 'I shall give you a new heart ... I shall remove the heart of stone from your bodies and give you a heart of flesh instead.' (Ezek 36:26)

The two foundation stones of their lives as missionaries

are to contemplate the love of God made visible and show his compassion to those who are in any need whatsoever. Contemplation is not looking at Jesus from the outside. It is engaging with him heart to heart. Cardinal Newman put it well when he said, '*Cor ad Cor loquitur*'. 'Heart speaks to heart in the silence of the Heart'. And it is this relationship with him which allows the missionary to express solidarity, compassion, suffering with those who are suffering, or marginalised, or dispossessed, or lonely, or lacking dignity or meaning in their lives.

It is to this love that our new Deacon commits himself today. Alan is called to have his own heart pierced so that the love of God can pour out for the weak, the poor, the hungry, the unborn and all his people. As a Deacon and a priest, his heart is no longer his own. That is why he will commit himself to celibacy 'for the sake of the kingdom'. His heart will burn with love for his local church, for his mission, for the people who will look to him as a personification of loving service. He knows he cannot do this alone. He in turn will need the love and support of his family, his friends and fellow missionaries. When he prostrates himself in front of the altar we pray that the example of the saints will inspire and sustain him in the gift he makes of himself to Christ and his Church. He will be clothed with diaconal vestments, not as a sign of power and authority, but to cover up his human frailty and to remind him that he is bound to and strengthened by the solidarity of the Order of Deacons which exists to 'serve at table'. He will be given the Book of the Gospels from which he will preach. But all of us who are ordained will tell him that there is more to preaching than standing in a pulpit, or indeed sitting in a chair. He must avoid the reminder of the English poet Edwin Muir who says, 'the word made flesh is here made word again'. He is not just to preach a spoken word, but a living word, Jesus living in him and he in Jesus. That is why he will take to heart the words of the Bishop in the *Traditio*, the handing on of the Gospels:

> Receive the Gospel of Christ, whose herald you now are.
> Believe what you read,
> Teach what you believe
> And practice what you teach.

Fr Keith Stoakes
Silver Jubilee
17 September 2008

Who could fail to be impressed with the three great missionary journeys undertaken by Pope Benedict this year? The first one to America in April, then the triumphant World Youth Day in Sydney in July, and just this weekend a visit to France and to Lourdes to celebrate the 150th anniversary of the appearance of Our Lady to Bernadette in that holy place. The talks and the sermons he gave on these visits are truly inspirational. They are well worth reading, perhaps even printed as sections in the parish newsletter week by week.

In the midst of this, the Pope has also declared this year to be a year dedicated to St Paul. He wants members of the Church to deepen our knowledge and understanding of who Paul is, and what his conversion and life and letters mean to us all today. At the Basilica of St Paul's Outside the Walls, Pope Benedict said:

> For us, St Paul is not a figure of the past whom we recall with veneration. He is our master, the apostle, the announcer of Jesus Christ to us too. His faith was the experience of being loved by Jesus Christ . . . It was an awareness of the fact that Christ died, faced death not for some unidentified cause, but for the love of him, of Paul, and that being risen, He loves him still. So Paul's faith was not a 'Theory'. It was the imprint of God's love on his heart.

So it is good on this Silver Jubilee Day that Fr Keith Stoakes takes Paul as his model for ministry and preaching. We listened to what Paul said in his letter to the Corinthians:

> Since we have been entrusted with this work of administration, there is no weakening on our part. On the contrary, we will have none of the reticence of those who are ashamed, no watering down of the word of God . . . For it is not ourselves that we are preaching but Christ Jesus as Lord, and ourselves as your servants for Jesus' sake. (2 Cor 4:5–7)

Don't those words reflect the experience we have of Keith's focus and fidelity as a priest over the last twenty-five years? Whatever parish and diocesan responsibilities he has been given he has fulfilled them, in the words of Paul, 'the way we commend ourselves to every human being is by stating the truth openly in the sight of God.'

In doing this, Keith has taken to heart and put into practice other beautiful words spoken by the Bishop in the Rite of Ordination when he gives the new priest bread and wine to be offered at Mass:

> Accept the gifts of the people to be offered to God. Be conscious of what you are doing. Be as holy as the actions you perform. Model your life after the mystery of the Lord's cross.

The Mass is the most obvious thing a priest does in the sight of God and in the sight of the people. Whatever else happens, the people have a right, and the priest has the duty, of celebrating Mass for the glory of God and the sanctification of the people. No wonder the Second Vatican Council said that the Eucharist is the source and summit of the life of the Church. When we receive Jesus in Holy Communion, we are also received *by* Jesus into Communion with him and with each other. That is why the building up of the Body of Christ which is the Church, which is the parish, is the constant privilege and responsibility of every priest. The priest is 'sent' to a parish so that he can be a sign of the constant presence and love of Jesus to every person, in season and out of season, in joyful times and in sad, to lead, to encourage, to teach, to correct and help them, help us, to bear one another's burdens, as the apostle Peter tells us. So the words of Jesus will be ringing in Keith's ears, and through his priesthood to all of us who receive his ministry: 'I call you friends, because I have made known to you everything I have learned from my Father'. (Jn 15:9–17)

The preaching, the catechetics, the prayer groups, the faith-sharing groups, the RCIA, the assemblies, the school Masses, the parish celebrations, the care for the sick, the comforting of the dying, all of these are ways in which we gradually learn the things that Jesus makes known to us, everything he has learned from his Father.

The Old Testament prophet Isaiah was speaking 2,500 years ago. He saw, like we do, a fragmented world around him. He realised that he and the people were called to be signs of reconciliation and healing and agents of change in an unjust world. So when people from every nation and background and understanding can come together Sunday by Sunday in this church to be signs of what our city, our society, our world should be, we realise that those words are addressed to each of us: 'The Lord sent me to bring good news to the poor. To bind up hearts that are broken. To comfort those who mourn. To proclaim a year of favour to our God'. (Is 61:1–3)

On Sunday Pope Benedict spoke to the Bishops of France in Lourdes. He quoted from Paul's letter to his young assistant Timothy to encourage him in preaching the Gospel. 'The time will surely come when, far from being content with sound teaching, people will be avid for the latest novelty and collect themselves a whole series of teachers according to their own taste'. Addressing Timothy directly he says: 'Be careful always to choose the right course. Be brave under trials. Make the preaching of the Good News your life's work, in thoroughgoing service'. (2 Tim. 4:3–4)

Thank you, Keith, for choosing the right path. Thank you for being brave under trials. Thank you for making the preaching of the Gospel your life's work and continuing to do so in thoroughgoing service, at least for the next twenty-five years!

Bishopric of the Forces
Chrism Mass
24 March 2009

As an outsider, the things that never fail to impress me about Her Majesty's Forces is the life of discipline, service, and fellowship which is at the heart of their common endeavour. In the midst of all the sophisticated equipment, logistics, dangers and dilemmas you have to face, it seems to me that it is the trust which is built up among those who serve which is the key to the whole undertaking.

That identity and trust cannot be dependent solely on individuals and their personalities. It has to transcend likes and dislikes, the prejudices and preferences we all have. The moulding together of people from different backgrounds and ages and outlooks is something in which the Forces are justifiably proud. You will know that this is done, in part, by a common language which unites you all. This language goes beyond words, it goes deeper than words. It is a language of sign and symbol, it speaks in a way that is understandable and accessible to all who commit themselves to it.

I think of the Oath of Allegiance, the Regimental Flag, the White Ensign, Procedure Alpha, the Battle of Britain Fly Past.

The priests who serve the men and women of the forces are familiar with this language long before they become chaplains. Because their lives, their vocation, their ministry can only be understood in a language of sign, symbol and sacrament. I love the words of Pope John Paul II when he said, 'They try to understand me from the outside in. I can only be understood from the inside out.' And then he communicated that truth when he could speak no longer in his public witness to the meaning of the cross in his own suffering and death.

The priests who serve our Forces continually point to a crucified Saviour. They remind those in their care that the Cross stands at the crossroads of human existence. That the burdens of life, its suffering and pain and, ultimately, death are not wasted in the sight of God. They preach that no time is wasted in which God is served. The service of God is the sanctification of time. And it is in times of perplexity and confusion, in times of weakness and sadness, that God in Jesus Christ nervously, tentatively invites us to embrace the Cross on which he himself overcame all the things that tempt us to doubt God's presence. On the Cross, Jesus does not withdraw God's love. He does not say, 'I have wasted my time. These people are unforgivable'. On the Cross, Jesus goes on revealing, goes on loving, goes on forgiving. Julian of Norwich puts it well in her vision of Jesus on the Cross. He says to her, 'If I could have done more, I would have done more.'

The priest is commissioned, directed, ordained to re-present that mystery, ultimately in the celebration of Mass. In the words of the Song of Songs, he is called to remind people that 'love is as strong as death'. In the celebration of the Sacraments, with each sign and gesture he makes, he repeats the words of the lover in that wonderful piece of scripture: 'Set me as a seal upon your heart'. He communicates to every person the dignity of his or her existence, and that the life of every individual is of infinite value and worth.

There will be times when the chaplain will find it hard to put these things into words. Perhaps that is most of the time. Not only in an age when the things of the Spirit are pushed to the margins, where the common language of faith and prayer, of history and tradition has to fight with so many words in the media, on computers, in training manuals and instructions. Far from communicating the truth, these words can often conceal or distort it.

That is why on this Chrism Mass day priests are asked to come together in solidarity, fellowship and communion. They are reminded, and so are the people, that we are not alone in this journey of faith. We take powerful symbols in the life of the Church that will speak to us in a wordless language about eternal truths.

The Oil of the Sick will be a comfort and support when health and strength are broken by sickness and pain, the fear of the unknown. The prayer of the Church and the anointing with oil will bring the one who is sick closest to the broken Heart of Jesus. Prayer for the sick and by the sick are powerful prayers indeed.

The Oil of Baptism is a symbol of the strength needed to be a person of faith, to be bound to Jesus Christ. It is a reminder to us that every baptised person is called to be a healer and reconciler in this fragile and broken world.

The Oil of Chrism is named after Christ, the anointed one. It is made of bittersweet oil, mixed as it is with balsam. That mixing is of a strange beauty: death and new life to be remembered each time we celebrate the Eucharist as God's priestly people.

No wonder priests are asked to renew their priestly promises today. They were not lightly made at ordination. They are songs of contradiction as we are told: 'Unite yourselves more fully to Christ by joyfully sacrificing your own pleasure and ambition to bring peace.' And then: 'Imitate Christ, the Head and the Shepherd by teaching the Christian faith for the well-being of the people you serve.' On the day of ordination, the new priest prostrated himself and was carried by the prayers of the people in the Litany of the Saints. Today, the people are asked: Pray for your priests that they may remain faithful ministers of Christ the High Priest.

Fr Peter O'Connor
Silver Jubilee
3 June 2009

As a child of the '60s, Peter O'Connor was influenced, as were so many of us, by the words and music of The Beatles. Imagine my surprise when on 3 June 1984 he gave me his ordination card, on one side of which was printed a reproduction of Leonardo da Vinci's 'The Last Supper'. On the other was printed the one word 'Imagine'. Was he trying to tell me, in John Lennon's words, 'Imagine there's no heaven. It's easy if you try. Imagine no hell below us. Above us only sky'?

Over the years I have come to understand and respect Peter's understanding of imagination. He loves the use of signs and symbols – especially in the liturgy and catechetics. His degree in Social Communications from Rome has developed his innate ability to explore the world of the visual arts and literature, the world of film and music. And over the years he has shared so many of his insights both through the spoken word on radio and television, and the written word in the various reviews and articles he has published in magazines and newspapers.

His imagination has led him to a practical knowledge and understanding of the work of the great twentieth-century psychologist, Carl Jung. Jung discovered the five great 'archetypes' of human life and thinking, explored and expressed in his theory of dreams. The symbolic, imaginative, world of dreams acts as a mirror from the subconscious to the conscious, integrating the landscape of our relationship with the outer world with the inner reality of who we are. Imagination is one of the tools which helps us build our integrity, a balance between body, mind and spirit. The psychologist calls this integrity 'wholeness'. In the Church, we call it holiness. Carl Jung developed the theme of the human person as *Imago Dei* the Image of God from the Book of Genesis. It is in the capacity of human beings to understand the reason why, to reflect and deliberate on our actions, to make choices as to what we do, which is the key as to how we reflect the creative action of God personally, socially, morally and spiritually.

That holiness is not easy to achieve or understand, not easy to put into words. Perhaps it is even more difficult in the age in which we live, when so many alternative, conflicting lifestyles and choices are put forward as constituting a good life. For us, the call to holiness is personified in the self-giving sacrifice of Jesus Christ to the point of death, and beyond. The language of sacrificial love depends not on words, but on actions. That is one reason why on that first Pentecost people could hear the message preached 'in their own language'. The truth about Jesus is a universal language, it goes beyond words. It goes deeper than words. It's an example and a challenge for us all.

We need to listen, perhaps experience, that language which is truth through the silent power of God's Spirit speaking to us. The great English Cardinal, John Henry Newman, described it as 'heart speaking to heart in the silence of the heart'. And we proclaim our faith in the abiding presence of Christ each time we come together and celebrate the Mystery of Faith: the Mass, the Eucharist, Holy Communion in which we re-member, put back together again, the broken members of His Body. 'In that day . . . I do not say that I will pray to the Father for you. For the Father loves you because you have loved the Father'.

None of us can do this alone, despite the gospel of individuality preached in our age. We are bound together in faith and baptism to be a communal sign that God's word is alive and active in us forming us as individuals and also as a worshipping community. Through faith and baptism we are empowered to worship God in *His* way, not merely human ways. That is why the Church calls us 'The Priestly People of God'. The one who is ordained, directed, focussed on these truths is called to be a sign, a sacrament himself, making it possible for the people to do their priestly duty. He is the priest of the priests of God.

> Imagine no possessions. I wonder if you can. No need for greed and hunger. A brotherhood of man. Imagine all the people. Sharing all the world. I hope some day you'll join us. And the world will be as one.

Not a bad agenda for the Church and the priesthood until Peter reaches the Golden Jubilee of his priesthood!

Imagination

There is a dish to hold the sea,
A brazier to contain the sun,
A compass for the galaxy,
A voice to wake the dead and done!

That minister of ministers,
Imagination, gathers up
The undiscovered Universe,
Like jewels in a jasper cup.

Its flame can mingle north and south;
Its accent with the thunder strive;
The ruddy sentence of its mouth
Can make the ancient dead alive.

The mart of power, the fount of will,
The form and mold of every star,
The source and bound of good and ill,
The key of all the things that are.

Imagination, new and strange
In every age, can turn the year;
Can shift the poles and lightly change
The mood of men, the world's career.

John Davidson
(1857 - 1909)

Fr Gerard O'Brien
First Mass
17 January 2010

First Reading: Isaiah 62:1–5
Second Reading: 1 Corinthians 12:4–11
Gospel: John 2:1–12

There is often a temptation in the Church to choose special scripture readings for important events to make them 'fit' the celebration we're having. It's a temptation I always resist and I'm glad that Fr Gerard has resisted it for the celebration of his First Mass today. What could be better than the readings given us for this Second Ordinary Sunday of the Church year? He will preach them many times in years to come. And what beautiful readings they are too.

The Wedding Feast of Cana in the Gospel of John. Being a scripture scholar, Gerard will know that there are many layers of meaning to this gospel passage. They need to be unravelled not just in a lecture or a sermon, but in life itself. John tells us that the changing of the water into wine was the first of seven 'signs' that Jesus worked. A sign points to something deeper. It is given for a reason. John tells us the reason for these signs at the end of his Gospel: '... so that you may believe that Jesus is the Christ, the Son of God, and that believing this you may have life through his name.' As Archbishop Nichols said during yesterday's Ordination, our new priest will use seven 'signs' in his ministry. We call them Sacraments. They are outward signs of inward grace ordained by Jesus Christ by which grace is given to the soul.

Gerard will celebrate those sacraments for people so that 'believing, they may have life through the name of Jesus.' In offering himself for service as a priest Gerard is already responding to the words of Mary to the servants at the wedding – and to us: 'Do whatever he tells you.' Many people will ask him to teach them how to pray. They will ask him to pray for them in their different needs. In his prayers Gerard will surely remember the words of Canon Michael Munnelly at the funeral of his father, Michael O'Brien, who didn't just pray *for* people but prayed *with* them too. What an example to follow!

It's no accident that the prophet Isaiah described the relationship between God and his people 2,500 years ago as a marriage:

> Like a young man marrying a virgin,
> So will God marry you;
> And as the bridegroom rejoices in his bride,
> So will God rejoice in you.

We've already had one ordination party and there'll be another one after this in the marquee. It's common knowledge that ordination parties are as good as any wedding reception (at least there aren't any fights!). In a special way, the priest is married to the Church which is the Bride of Christ. He is called father of the family because his job is to nourish and feed and nurture God's people with Word, Sacrament and with his life. He will do this not through power and control but by holding up a mirror to people's lives and letting them see the image of their dignity as the people of God. Having seen that, they will recognise that each one is infinitely loveable, infinitely forgivable in the sight of God. In his ministry he will help people release their gifts of love and life, of service and healing and forgiveness. That is what Paul was talking about in the second reading. St Irenaeus put it differently in the second century, 'The glory of God is humanity fully alive.'

In one of the great solemn moments of yesterday's Ordination ceremony the Archbishop gave to the new priest the chalice and patten with the bread and wine. What a wonderful spiritual bond with Bishop Jim O'Brien whose chalice is now given to another Fr O'Brien. He 'handed it on' (*traditio instrumentorum*).

> Accept from the holy people of God the gifts to be offered to him.
> Know what you are doing, and imitate the mystery you celebrate.
> Model your life on the mystery of the Lord's cross.

Gerard will receive those gifts again during today's Offertory procession. And amongst the many things he will do is pour a drop of water into the rich wine of the chalice reflecting the miracle of Cana. He will say in his turn:

> By the mystery of this water and wine
> May we come to share in the divinity of Christ
> Who humbled himself to share in our humanity.

In the Sacrament of the Holy Communion which we will receive during Gerard's First Mass we will give thanks with St John and say:

> . . . we believe that Jesus is the Christ, the Son of God, and that believing this we have life through his name.

That is the end of my official sermon. But how could I finish without paying tribute to Ann & Michael for the gift of Gerard to the Church of God? Without paying tribute to Joseph the fisherman, to David my youth club leader, to John my Altar Server, to my favourite punkette and to Bernadette: *Semper fidelis* (your gift will be repaid) by the countless people who will learn to know and love God through the mystery of Gerard your son, your brother, our friend.

Amen.

Fr Joseph Ryan
Fortieth Anniversary of Priestly Ordination
11 June 2011

First Reading: Jeremiah 1:4–8
Second Reading: 1 Corinthians 12:4–11
Gospel: Luke 10:1–9

Almost twenty years ago, I was one of the Directors of the company set up by the Diocese of Westminster to buy the freehold of the Silver Lady Pub next door to the church. Eventually it became the parish centre, a real phoenix rising from the ashes of the wooden hall that had been burned down a few years before. Since then, I have always thought of the church of St John Vianney and the Phoenix Centre being like two lungs which breathe life into the Body of Christ here in West Green parish. You are alive and active not just for your own good but for the service of the wider community of this part of Haringey and beyond.

But I really am disappointed that in the midst of all the wonderful activities which take place here, the Phoenix Centre no longer holds Bingo sessions! Those of us who worship at the Temple of Bingo will know that Blind Forty, or naughty forty, or more significantly 'life begins at forty' are all clues as to how important the number forty is, whichever way you look at it. It's important in the Bible too. Moses led the People of Israel in their search for the Promised Land for forty years. Noah saved his people and his animals from the flood by building an ark and sailing for forty days until the flood subsided. And Jesus spent forty days and forty nights in the desert, being tempted, being challenged, as to what kind of Messiah he would be. How was he really going to unfold God's saving plan to the people of his time and ours too?

The recent banking crisis has reminded us that we all still live with those temptations. Free credit and huge debts made sure, when they were recalled, that the banks would be baled out by the taxpayers. Although we failed to count the cost, we guaranteed that those who persuaded us to live beyond our means would not dash their foot against a stone. The invitation to 'fall down and worship me' doesn't just relate to statues and idol worship. Pope Benedict spoke very clearly about the devilish pact we make with wealth and money.

What has all that got to do with Fr Joe Ryan and the fortieth anniversary of his priesthood? Having known him for virtually the whole of his priestly life, I can say that he has been a prophetic voice, not just in word but in his actions proclaiming: 'Live simply so that others may simply live'. His commitment to those who are poor in any way whatsoever is an expression of this. His passion and compassion for justice, truth and integrity has been lived out in public high profile campaigns and in quiet, private, personal concern for the dignity and well-being of so many individual people. The people of this parish will know at first hand of his capacity to develop confidence and responsibility, helping them as individuals and as a community to make a difference to the world in which they live. He truly believes that 'There are a variety of gifts, but always the same Spirit. There are all sorts of services to be done, but always to the same Lord, working in all sorts of different ways in different people.'

The readings chosen for this Jubilee Mass say it all. Like all priests, in his heart of hearts Joe echoes the words of the prophet Jeremiah, knowing that on his own he is not capable of going into the most unexpected places and proclaiming God's word and God's way. At his ordination in the Cathedral at Thurles, forty years ago, Joe placed his trust in God and became part of the band of missionaries we read about in Luke's Gospel: 'He sent them out two by two to all the towns he himself was to visit'. (Luke 10:1) How good it is to have Joe's friend, Fr John Beatty, with us today. These two were ordained on the same day and we would want to congratulate John and thank him on his fortieth anniversary as well.

* * *

This is my last engagement in the Diocese of Westminster after nearly forty years here serving as a Bishop, Priest and Deacon. I am driving to Cardiff straight after this Mass. One reason I didn't cancel this engagement is that I hope Joe will preach at my fortieth anniversary of priesthood next year! But my real reason is that I can think of no better example of priestly dedication and service, of humility and simplicity of life, of solidarity and prophetic witness that he offers to himself, to his fellow priests, to this parish and to the wider Church. I feel privileged to be here to give thanks to God with you for this good and faithful priest.

Rt Rev Peter Brignall
Episcopal Ordination
Third Bishop of Wrexham
12 September 2012

During the retreat which precedes Episcopal ordination, the candidate becomes painfully aware of his unworthiness for the office to which he is called. He reads the scriptures, reflects on the teaching of the Church, and embraces the tradition. He realises that, humanly speaking, this ministry cannot depend on his gifts alone, but on the power and the grace of the Holy Spirit which breathes through the Body of Christ which is the Church.

During his reflection, Bishop-Elect Peter may even have found himself in agreement with the words of Blessed Humbert of Rome (c. 1190–1277). Humbert was the fifth successor of Dominic as Master of the Dominicans. He remonstrated with his teacher St Albert the Great who had been appointed a Bishop:

> I would rather you were dead than a Bishop . . . Why ruin your reputation and that of the Order by letting yourself be taken away from poverty and preaching? However troublesome you find the brethren, do not imagine that things will be better when you have the clergy and the secular powers to deal with. . . . Better to lie in a coffin that sit in a Bishop's chair!

Peter's missionary spirit led him away, not from the Dominicans but from the Diocese of Westminster to Wrexham in 1977. Cardinal Hume allowed him to leave on condition 'that he didn't take anyone else with him'. He didn't take me with him from Westminster at that time, but thirty-five years later I have followed the call of

St David, and am now privileged with him and Bishop Tom Burns to serve God's people here in Wales. Peter's distinguished ministry as a parish priest, hospital chaplain, chaplain to the deaf, university chaplain, Dean of the Cathedral and Vicar General are just some examples of his willingness and capacity to be of service wherever he is needed. 'Watch over the flock God has entrusted to you, not simply as a duty but gladly ... because you are eager to do it'. (1 Peter 5:2)

Before his ordination, the new Bishop is asked publicly and personally if he is willing to undertake this service for the glory of God and the salvation of God's people. 'Are you resolved to maintain the deposit of faith? Are you resolved to build up the Church? Are you resolved to be united to the successor of Peter? To be compassionate? To be a good shepherd and above all to pray with and for the People of God?' He accepts the mandate given to every bishop to sanctify, to teach and to govern when he answers: 'I am, with the help of God.'

The Sacrament of Orders is conferred through the laying on of hands and prayer. The imposition of hands by all the bishops happens in silence. The human word is inarticulate. The soul opens in silence to God whose hand stretches from eternity into the world of time and embraces this man, directs and orders him for service of the whole Body which is the Church. And then the prayer of consecration. Pope Benedict reminds us, 'No man can make another man a priest or a bishop. It is the Lord himself who, through these sacramental signs and prayer, draws a man into His own priesthood'. Through his ministry as Bishop, Peter will make the priesthood of Christ visible in this place, at this time and for these people in the changing circumstances of the world in which we live.

The symbols of Episcopal office speak in a silent language of the presence of Christ in his Church particularly when it is gathered around the Bishop in worship. The anointing of his head with the Oil of Chrism, sealing the bond between Christ and his new apostle. 'The spirit of the Lord has been given to me, for the Lord has anointed me' said the prophet Isaiah (61:1). The mitre represents a crown of holiness in life and in ministry. It is also a reminder that holiness cannot by-pass the crown of thorns, the crown of suffering in any of our lives. And the Bishop's staff – a sign of direction and hope. Reaching out to those in any need whatsoever and a reminder that he himself has to be supported and upheld by the Prayer of the Church.

The *Cathedra* gives its name to this Cathedral. It is not just any old chair. It is the seat of teaching, listening and learning. In his role as teacher the Bishop is called to speak God's word. The Word is not his own. No matter what their background, outlook, upbringing, point of view, people are gathered around their Bishop in unity, identity and communion with God and with each other. The *Cathedra* is a holy place.

Bearing all that in mind, Bishop Peter may well have reflected in his retreat on the words of the fifth-century Bishop, St Augustine of Hippo. On the anniversary of his ordination Augustine preached:

> When I am fearful of what I am for you
> I draw strength from what I am with you.
> For you, I am a Bishop.
> With you, I am a Christian.
> The former is an office received.
> The latter is the foundation of salvation.
> Help me by your prayers and obedience
> To carry out these serious and varied duties.
> Then I shall have the joy
> Not so much of ruling you
> As of being useful to your salvation.

Canon Joseph Boardman Silver Jubilee Mass 2 July 2013

TV programs like 'Who do you think you are?' and 'The Heir Hunters' remind us that genealogy is a growing industry in this country! Memories are short. Our grand-parents' photo albums can't tell the whole story. We need pictures to be brought to life by a word or story about the black sheep of the family.

Memory is an important word in the life of the Church. Ours is a sacramental religion. We believe that God has revealed himself to us not just in words, not just telling us about himself, but by coming among us and sharing our life so that we might share his life.

So Catholics don't just read the Bible, or say our prayers, or listen to sermons. We don't tell God things he obviously doesn't know about the human condition. God is a poet and an artist who can use material in ways that human poets and artists cannot. As creator of all, God can transform and re-create the elements and realities of this world so that they can become the elements and realities of the Kingdom of Heaven. So with water and wine. Bread and oil. Birth and maturity. Sickness and betrayal. Community and eating. Marriage and teaching. All these human elements and realities become instruments of God's presence in a sacramental religion such as ours. This is where we meet God, not as some intellectual abstraction, but as the Word made Flesh.

It is quite difficult to remember and experience those things in a busy life. The Second Vatican Council spoke of 'the joys and hopes' and the sorrows and anguish of our world. (*Gaudium et Spes*) When we are worn down by suffering, sickness, problems, death itself, words fail us. Jesus, the poet of human life and death, doesn't just speak about these things. He enters into the depth of human pain and misunderstanding. Where is God in the midst of human confusion and pain? 'Here', says Jesus, with arms outstretched on the Cross. And because none of us ever really learns how to understand the mystery of suffering, Jesus took bread and wine the night before he died and said, 'Take and eat. My body. My blood. Given for you. Do this in memory of me'.

There is really only one priest, Jesus Christ. There is really only one sacrifice, his death on the cross. There is really only one prayer, the intercession he makes eternally in the presence of God. Yet we call ourselves a 'priestly people' and call those ordained to serve this people as 'priests'. We dare to say that because, by God's grace, we are privileged to make visible Christ's work of redeeming the world. We dare to call ourselves members of the Body of Christ because he said 'where two or three are gathered in my name I am there among you'. John's Gospel puts it poetically, 'I am the vine, you are the branches'. (John 15:5) We are called priests because of the communion we have with Christ the High Priest and worship God in his way, not our own.

Actions speak louder than words. 'This is what I received from the Lord and in turn passed on to you'. Paul didn't just give the Christians at Corinth a list of instructions. He re-presented the actions of Jesus. Not just at the table, but in his missionary journeys, in his preaching, in his imprisonment and in his martyrdom. We need to re-member, put back together again, the words and the actions of the Eucharist. Not just the spoken words, but all they signify in terms of passion and compassion. If God is a poet, is it too much to say that the ordained priest is his 'poet in residence', personifying the saving mystery in which we all believe but which has to be expressed in communion? In a few minutes we will sing:

> Take all that daily toil plants in our heart's poor soil
> Take all we start and spoil, each hopeful dream.
> The chances we have missed.
> The graces we resist,
> Lord in thy Eucharist
> Take and redeem.

Thank you, Joe, for transforming the joys and hopes, the dreams and visions, the sufferings and sadnesses of countless thousands of people you have served as a priest in the last twenty-five years. Your Silver Jubilee is half a Jubilee in the Biblical sense of fifty. But ours is a religion of hope as well as faith. Who knows what the next twenty-five years will bring!

Sr Imelda McKenna
Golden Jubilee
6 June 2004

It was the best of times;
  it was the worst of times.
It was the age of wisdom;
  it was the age of foolishness.
It was the epoch of belief;
  it was the epoch of incredulity.
It was the season of Light;
  it was the season of Darkness.
It was the spring of hope;
  it was the winter of despair.
We had everything before us;
  we had nothing before us.
We were all going direct to Heaven;
  we were all going direct the other way.

Words of Charles Dickens, taken from his novel *A Tale of Two Cities*. It was written about a time in history when the heart of Europe seemed to be torn from its body. It was called the Age of Enlightenment, the Age of Reason, an age when the things of God were to take second place in people's hearts. A time, perhaps, not unlike our own.

It was in the midst of that revolutionary turmoil that the life of the child who would become the foundress of the Daughters of the Cross was forged. One of seven children, Marie Therese was the victim of the familiar story of 'minor aristocrats' who became the object of revolutionary hatred. Moving from place to place, parents separated from children suffering from the inevitable decline into poverty. Yet growing up in these worst of times, something of the best was being formed in Marie Therese. It was in 1820 that she formalised what had always been in her heart. A dedication to care for the poor, to educate the illiterate, to teach the ways of Jesus to those who had been deprived of religious life on the altar of reason.

We would call the charism, which became the foundation of the life of her new congregation, an 'option for the poor'. The constitution by which the Sisters live makes clear that they 'will always have a special preference for those who are poorest. They will serve Christ in the work of education, care of the sick and the aged, abandoned children, the physically and mentally deprived and the various needs of the Church.'

How can they do this, both as individuals and as members of a community? The constitution again:

> By encountering Jesus and being united to Him as He prays to His Father through the Spirit.
> By taking to heart the words of the scriptures and contemplating him whose death on the cross offers life.
> By sharing in the Eucharist which unites the members of this congregation to each other and the whole Church.

Isn't it marvellous that we celebrate this Golden Jubilee of the religious profession of Sr Imelda on the Feast of the Most Holy Trinity? The Trinity is the ultimate community of love which is the centre of our religion. The author of the Book of Proverbs might have been thinking of Imelda when he describes wisdom as delighting in God, day after day, ever at play in his presence, everywhere in this world, delighting to be with the sons of men.

Delight is a word I associate with Imelda and her faithfulness to her vocation. Delight in her teaching. Delight in poetry. Delight in art. In contemplation. Delight in the beauty of creation. Delight in people which I came to know so well in her helping them on their journey of faith through the RCIA at Westminster Cathedral. Haven't we all been surprised by joy with the gift of a beautiful picture here, a lovely prayer there, a piece of poetry, a text in marvellous calligraphy, something Imelda has found useful and wishes to share with others.

That wonder and awe, that delight and contemplation is at the heart of Imelda's life as a Daughter of the Cross. Why? Because of Paul's proclamation that suffering brings patience. Patience brings perseverance. Perseverance brings hope. Not just 'hoping for the best' but the conviction that the love of God has been poured into our hearts by the Holy Spirit. And on this Trinity Sunday, Jesus promises that his Spirit will tell Imelda, and each of us, of the things to come. 'In becoming sensitive to the prayer of the Spirit within us, the Daughter of the Cross allows herself to be transformed by it'.

Sr Imelda would expect me to finish with a piece of poetry, so I won't disappoint her. I can think of nothing better than T.S. Eliot's 'Choruses from the Rock' when he says:

> What life have you, if you have not life together?
> There is no life that is not in community,
> And no community not lived in praise of God.
> Even the anchorite who meditates alone,
> For whom days and nights repeat the praise of God,
> Prays for the Church, the Body of Christ Incarnate.

www.ingramcontent.com/pod-product-compliance
Lightning Source LLC
Chambersburg PA
CBHW031323040426
42443CB00005B/200

* 9 7 8 0 8 5 2 4 4 8 4 5 8 *